ANGELS CALLING

ANGELS CALLING

50 Invitations to Energize Your Life

Anselm Gruen

Translated by
Dinah Livingstone

Translated & edited by
Gwendolin Herder

A CROSSROAD BOOK
The Crossroad Publishing Company
New York

The Crossroad Publishing Company
www.crossroadpublishing.com

First published in Great Britain in 1998 by
Burns & Oates

Original Edition *50 Engel für das Jahr*
Published by Verlag Herder GmbH & Co. KG
Freiburg, Germany
© Verlag Herder Freiburg im Breisgau 1997

English Translation © 2009 by The Crossroad Publishing Company

In continuation of our 200-year tradition of independent publishing, The Crossroad Publishing Company proudly offers a variety of books with strong, original voices and diverse perspectives. The viewpoints expressed in our books are not necessarily those of The Crossroad Publishing Company, any of its imprints or of its employees. No claims are made or responsibility assumed for any health or other benefit.
Photo credits: title page–Giovanni Dall'Orto; page 93–Carelmare

Printed in China.

Library of Congress Cataloging-in-Publication Data
Grün, Anselm.
    [50 Engel für das Jahr. English]
    Angels calling : 50 invitations to energize your life / by Anselm Gruen.
        p. cm.
    Originally published: New York : Crossroad Pub. Co., 1998.
    ISBN-13: 978-0-8245-2571-2 (alk. paper)
    ISBN-10: 0-8245-2571-X (alk. paper)
    ISBN-13: 978-0-8245-1761-8 (alk. paper)
    ISBN-10: 0-8245-1761-X (alk. paper)
    1. Angels--Meditations. I. Title.
    BT966.3.G7813 2009
    235'.3--dc22
                                          2009045256
1 2 3 4 5 6 7 8 9 10   15 14 13 12 11 10 09

TABLE OF CONTENTS

INTRODUCTION

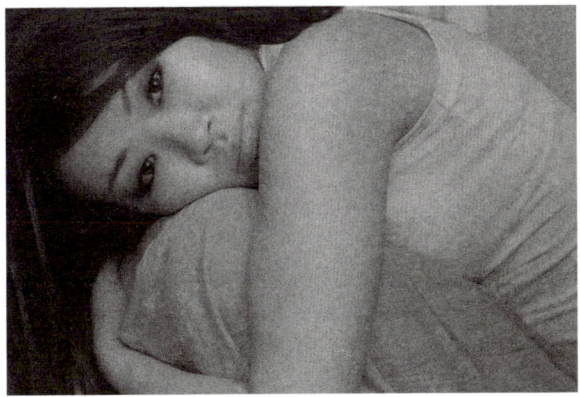

A young woman is at a New Year's
Eve party. She is among a circle of people
who want to begin the year with a sense
of awareness, not just with champagne and
fireworks. Someone has written fifty *angels
for the year* on fifty cards, and the players
are invited to pick for themselves an angel
for the coming year. Each card has an attitude written on it, representing an approach
to life.

Of course not all fifty attitudes can determine my life at once. But when I adopt one attitude for a whole year, then that will have an effect on my whole life, something new will happen in me. An attitude can be something to hold on to through life's insecurity. It corresponds to what used to be called a virtue. *Virtus*, the Latin word for virtue, means both power and strength. Virtue is a power that can transform our life. The Greek word for virtue was *arete*, meaning the character of a noble and formed person. In German the word for virtue, *Tugend*, comes from the verb *taugen*, meaning to be good for something. So when we exercise a virtue, then our life is good for something, it will succeed.

The attitudes on the cards at that party were related to angels. Today angels have become modern again. For years they held a modest place in theology and the people's general awareness, but today they are once again treated with respect in countless books. In the Bible angels are God's messengers.

They indicate that God is at hand to help and heal. It is not always clear whether they are independent beings or just images of God's loving and comforting presence. But what is certain is that angels are heralds of another, deeper reality for human beings. We associate them with beautiful images, imaginings, and yearnings for another world of security and light, beauty, and hope. Part of the deep truth about angels is that they show us there is more to our life, that it relates to something beyond ourselves. Angels are images of the deep-seated, constant longing for help and healing, which does not come from ourselves. The fact that they are "in" again today expresses a hope: that our lives are not really empty, that we can succeed, we can live up to our real aspirations. Angels are spiritual traveling companions. They bring us in touch with a desire that each of us has deep down. They are a source of inspiration. They breathe another, larger life into us that goes with this longing in our hearts.

God sends his angels to protect people. In childhood we were taught the prayer to our guardian angel. Many adults have given up the image of a guardian angel. But when they have a lucky escape from a car accident, they still believe a guardian angel saved them. It is not important whether it was God himself who protected us, or an angel sent by him. Images have their own power. So we can confidently use the language of images to describe God's helping action. There are angels who stand by us. Angels watch over us. Angels speak to us in dreams to tell us which way to go.

Angels are traveling companions. They show us the way, just as the angel Raphael once led young Tobias safely to his destination. God sent his angel to free Peter from prison and to strengthen Jesus on the Mount of Olives. Angels often tell us what we do not understand. An angel told Mary what would happen to her. An angel appeared to Joseph in a dream to explain what was going on with Mary, his betrothed. Today angels are back with us again. The poet Rilke often writes of angels who come into our lives. Modern artists paint pictures of angels. Paul Klee painted angels in his later years. In 1920 he painted the famous Angelus Novus. Marc Chagall painted the Angel in Paradise. Salvador Dali painted the Angel, and there are many others. Even pop music has taken up angels: there are at least five songs titled simply *Angel*, (by Rod Stewart, Aretha Franklin, Madonna, Aerosmith, and The Eurythmics), three *Angel of the Morning*, (P. P. Arnold, Juice Newton, and Mary Mason); there are *Angel Faces*, *Angel Eyes*, and even *Angel Fingers*. Today many people connect the ideas of protection, security, beauty, hope, and light with angels.

The Scriptures say something else about angels. Angels see God's face. In the words of Jesus: "See that you do not despise one of these little ones. For I tell you that in heaven their angels always behold the face of my

Father" (Matt. 18:10). St Benedict, the sixth-century founder of Western monasticism, was convinced that monks sing the psalms in the sight of God's angels. They do not sing alone. Angels stand around them and open heaven to their song. Angels bear their prayers to God. They give people hope and confidence that these prayers are not in vain. Angels, who stand around us when we pray, join heaven and earth. They are beside us, so that we are not here alone praying to God with our troubles. Angels tell us: God is near. You are bathed in his healing and loving presence.

The idea that angels correspond to particular attitudes has been adopted by the Findhorn community in Scotland. The people in this community are convinced that we can come to an understanding with angels, that angels tell us something about ourselves and our capacity for change. They give us support and imbue us with new attitudes. These are the kind of angels we mean with this book's *fifty angels for the year.*

They are angels who lead us into attitudes that do us good in our lives.

These angels want to bring out something in us, something we may forget or set aside in our busy everyday lives. It is a beautiful idea to imagine that this year I will be accompanied by the angel of faithfulness or the angel of tenderness, that God sends me an angel who will introduce me into the secret of faithfulness or tenderness. The fifty angels in this book are calling us, offering to be companions on our life's journey. They are messengers of hope that our lives have purpose and that we can reach the goals of our lives. The fifty attitudes describe powers to shape our lives, to transform them, so that we increasingly match the *original picture*: how we could and should be. Angels represent our potential for transformation and calling them angels refers, of course, to the fact that these attitudes are never only the expression of our own efforts. They are also gifts of grace and wisdom that are given to us.

At the New Year's Eve party, each player drew an angel. They each believed they had picked the very angel they needed for the New Year, to do them good. We could also wish a friend an angel for a birthday or name day. The thoughts we had about an individual angel might help us make our good wishes more concrete. Then the greetings on the card we send will be more than empty words. You can also choose an angel for yourself, to accompany you for the coming week, the coming month, or at the New Year.

Choose the angel you need, the one you believe will do you good just now. And if you like, you can share your experience with others you know also living with an angel. What has your angel taught you? What experiences have you had with your angel? What new things have happened? What has started moving? What has blossomed in you?

THE ANGEL OF LOVE

LOVE IS SUCH AN OVERUSED WORD that I am wary of putting it at the beginning of the list of fifty angels. Pop songs sing about love. Everything revolves around love. Many people wrongly connect love with the idea of fulfilled sexuality. But however much the word is abused, in the depths of our heart every one of us longs for love. We want someone to love us unconditionally.

We are happy when we fall in love with someone who returns our love. Then something blossoms inside us. Joy streams from our face. We know we are unconditionally accepted and loved. Love—as fairy tales tell us—can bring back to life people who have turned to stone. It can turn animals back into human beings. It can make people who are dominated by an instinct (this is the meaning of represented by animals in fairy tales), people who are put under a spell by a witch turn back into beautiful princes or princesses. They become lovable and desirable people again, people who can be happy and make other people happy.

If I wish the Angel of Love for myself or for you, I am not only wishing that you may be loved or that you fall in love with a man or a woman. Love is more than being in love. For me love is a quality of the self. In my cell I have an icon of St. Nicholas. When I look at it, I feel that this saint is all love. Love simply shines out of him. He is not in love with a woman. Probably he is

not in love with Jesus Christ either, but he is
so imbued with love that he reflects it back
with his whole being. This is a fundamental human longing, not only to love another
man or woman but actually to become love.
When you become love, you love everything
around you. You greet every human being
with love and draw love out of them. You
treat every blade of grass with respect and
love. You know that, as the Talmud says,
God has given every blade of grass an angel, to make it grow. You look at the setting
sun with love. You feel that you are loved by
God, and that God's love streams through
you. Everything you do is marked by this
love. You do your work for love. If you sing,
you sing because you love, because your
love seeks expression.

People have always connected love with
angels. To anyone who loves me I say: you
are an angel. If I experience love, I have the
feeling that an angel has come into my life.
We need angels of love, to lead us into love's
mystery, to put us in touch with the spring of

love bubbling up in us, but which is one often trapped or muddied by our sick emotions.

But you have to go carefully with the Angel of Love. You should not demand too much of her. She can only transform the material you offer her. If you repress and block your aggressive feelings, the Angel cannot penetrate them with its her love. They remain in you like bitter coffee grounds. And gradually they will ruin all your efforts to love. Offer your Angel of Love everything that is in you, including your trouble and your anger, your jealousy and fear, your weariness and disappointment, because everything in you can be transformed by love. Let the Angel of Love accompany you in everything. Take it with you into your conflicts at work, your family quarrels, marriage, and friendships. The Angel of Love is not a sort of pious icing to spread over everything; it wants to transform your life. It forbids you nothing. It does not forbid you to feel annoyed. It does not demand you should not feel hurt. It only wants you to allow it to shine through everything you experience. Then you will see your conflicts in another light. They will not just disappear. There will not always be quick and easy solutions. But you will see the problems more clearly. Your Angel of Love loves truth. It wants you to look clearly honestly at what has happened. This includes, to taking seriously what you feel in any conflict. But it also wants you not to cling on to your injured feelings, but let them be tested by love.

First and foremost, loving does not mean having loving feelings. The word 'love' is related to the Old Saxon word *liob*, meaning dear or precious. It requires belief and the ability to see that something or someone is precious or good, in order to love and be able to treat him or her well. So loving requires a new way of seeing. Ask your Angel of Love to give you new eyes, so that you can see the people around you and yourself in a new light and discover the precious core in yourself and others. Then you will be able to treat yourself and others more kindly. My wish for you is that your Angel of Love may lead you deeper and deeper into the mystery of divine love, which is like a spring in you that never fails. You do not have to create love in yourself. You have only to drink at the spring of divine love, which is bubbling up in you and is always enough.

THE ANGEL
OF RECONCILIATION

FIRST OF ALL, The Angel of Reconciliation should enable you first of all to become reconciled to yourself. Today it is easy for us not to be at peace with ourselves. Then we cannot reconcile ourselves to the fact that our lives have turned out differently from the way we planned them. We at odds with our fate and the disappointments life has brought us. We are at war with ourselves. We cannot accept ourselves. We would like to be different, more intelligent, successful, and lovable. We would like to look better. We have a distinct image of ourselves, one that we can't live up to.

The word 'reconcile' comes via Old French from the Latin word *reconcilare*, meaning to bring back into friendly relations, just as the German word Versohnung comes from Middle High German sfiene, meaning mediation, peace, and kiss. There is also a sense of calming and making still evoked by this word. So reconciling myself means to make peace with myself, to come to terms with myself as I am now, to resolve the conflict between the different needs and wishes that drive me hither and thitherhere and there, to heal the split between my ideal self-image and my reality, to calm the angry soul that keeps resisting my reality. It means kissing embracing what I find so difficult, my faults and weaknesses, treating myself tenderly, especially that whatever in me that contradicts my ideal self-image. For this I need the help of an angel, so that I succeed in becoming reconciled to myself, so that I can really say yes to my life story, my character, and to all the baggage I have acquired on my way.

Only when I am reconciled with myself can I think about reconciling with people around me, who are at odds with me or with others. People who are divided and unreconciled with themselves will also cause division around them. Today there are many pious people, who conceal the split within themselves. Because they have too high a self-image, they split off the dark side of themselves. They have to project this onto others, so they continually see the devil or some demon in other people. They demonize those who do not live by the religious rules, that who do not correspond to their idea of morality. Because they have split off the devil in their own heart, they see him everywhere outside of their heart. These people cause division around them.

Sometimes they are regarded enthusiastically — as people who are confident of telling the truth. Others feel that something sick and divisive emanates from people like this, and they turn away. The Apostle Paul understands Christian service precisely as a service of reconciliation. God has taken upon himself the service of reconciliation (cf. 2 Cor. 5:18). The Angel of Reconciliation wants to make you a messenger of reconciliation, not because you go about preaching and demanding that people around you become reconciled, but because you bring reconciliation. Reconciliation does not mean covering up all the conflicts around you with a cloak of piety, or that you have to iron out every difference of opinion and every disagreement. Many people confuse this with reconciliation. But really, people do this because they cannot cope with conflicts. They are afraid if everything is not harmonious around them. They are reminded of situations in their childhoods that made them feel insecure, such as marital quarrels, which were threatening to them because they these experiences took away their feeling of safety at home. Reconciliation means peace-making. And peace-making means clearing the way, building a bridge between quarrelling groups. It does not mean smoothing everything over, making everything harmonious. Different points of view must remain. But the fighting can end. There is a bridge by which the parties can again communicate, by which they can reach each other.

Before you try to reconcile others, before you can make peace in a quarrel between hostile groups, you must become reconciled with yourself. And you must live at peace with the people around you. This does not mean that you must sacrifice all your feelings and needs for the sake of peace. On the contrary, if you suppress your annoyances for the sake of peace, you will never become really truly reconciled with what has annoyed you. You must take your feelings seriously and you must not judge your feelings. Feelings all have meaning. If you get become annoyed with a colleague at work, this is for a reason. Annoyance is the impulse to change something or see something differently. If I get annoyed when I am talking to someone and then piously suppress my annoyance, this poisons the atmosphere. If I express my annoyance appropriately, without judging it, this annoyance can clarify something. Annoyance often shows that the other person is not really being honest or forthright but and is speaking in a roundabout way. If I express my annoyance, I give the other person the opportunity for self-criticism. I build a bridge between us, by means of which and we can communicate better and more honestly. But it is crucial that I do not insist on being right. I must also respect the other person and try to become reconciled. Reconciliation means taking the other person seriously, but also taking myself and my feelings seriously.

Reconciliation has a political dimension. Unreconciled people divide not only the people around them. The division goes further. It forms opinion in an entire country. It confirms prejudices against others who think differently or live differently. It creates an atmosphere of violence against foreigners and people who behave in a foreign way. So the Angel of Reconciliation wants to turn you into a leaven of reconciliation for our world. If you speak peacefully, reconciliation will come from you. Then foreigners outsiders and marginal groups around you will feel accepted. You will not sow split peas but seeds of hope and reconciliation.

THE ANGEL OF EXUBERANCE

I FIND THE WORD 'EXUBERANCE' rather off-putting, maybe because I am a controlled rather than exuberant person. But perhaps, like me, you could do with a bit of exuberance. Being exuberant or unrestrained means letting go of my persona, the role I usually play, dropping the mask and giving outward expression to the liveliness within me. We call exuberant persons high-spirited. Their mood and their spirits are higher than normal. They do not live according to the normal habit of the daily grind, but with their own strenuous energy. Their heart is overflowing with the joy of life.

The Angel of Exuberance can give you the courage to trust your own liveliness. You must not always worry about what other people think of you or whether what you are doing conforms with the usual custom and meets other people's expectations. You should just trust yourself and your own heart. Life wants to express itself. And life does not always flow along evenly. It can bubble over with high spirits and be childish and spontaneous. You can't just decide that now you will be spontaneous. That would be a contradiction. Either you are spontaneous or you are not. When you force yourself to be spontaneous, then you have already ceased to be so.

Perhaps you are highly just disciplined. If so, you could ask the Angel of Exuberance to lead you to freedom. It requires distance from ourselves to allow ourselves simply to live as we feel. Too often we consider what other people will think, what impression we  will make on others, if we behave in such and such a manner. Exuberance is freedom from worrying over other people's expectations. We set aside these expectations and trust to the life that is in us. We let go of the role we usually play. We drop the mask, which often represses our inner bounce.

Exuberance means sparkling liveliness. We cannot force it. Sometimes we feel lively. Everything pours out of us. Words just bubble up and out of us. Our mood is infectious, and everybody catches it. We have silly daft notions. This kind of exuberance often inspires others. And it feels free. Other people also feel free for once to trust their own intuitions, the child in them that wants to play, without asking why or what is the use. This child is in touch with itself. It lives for itself and not in accordance with the expectations of other people. When we are grown-up, we long simply to live like this again. We want to stop making life so complicated by worrying over what we can and should do and what other people want. My wish for you is that the Angel of Exuberance may lead you into this childlike freedom, so that you can enjoy life and freedom with all your senses.

THE ANGEL OF SAFEKEEPING

6 'SAFEKEEPING' MEANS AWARENESS, respect, supervision, and care. It means that we are aware and careful about everything we experience: what we hear, see, and know. In our rushing lives we need the Angel of Safekeeping, not to keep us in the past, but so that we do not lose the treasure of our experience in the hectic pace of life. In our fast-paced times we often lose

sight of what we have seen. We flit from one impression to another. This means nothing can grow in us. We feel torn. We cannot properly taste what we have experienced. Today many people are incapable of living intensely in the present, of feeling what they experience. So they constantly need more external stimuli to feel be aware of themselves at all.

The old monks developed a method of living completely in the present. This was the method of meditation, or as they also called it, ruminatio. To ruminate means to chew over. So they took the words from scripture into their mouth and kept chewing them over. They repeated them in their hearts, considered and reconsidered them, looked at the word from all sides. They could take spend a whole day over one word of scripture. The word became flesh in them. It changed them. It gave them something to hold onto in their spiritual unrest and the noisy world. It enabled them to live completely for the moment. Nothing was more important for them than to be present in the presence of God.

The Church Fathers had a saying, which comparinged the behavior of horses and camels. The camel, they said, is content with little food, which it keeps chewing over. But the horse needs a lot to eat. It is never satisfied. St. Anthony advises us not to be a like a horse but like a camel with the word of God. We should not keep stuffing ourselves greedily with more but keep the little we have heard and read in our hearts. Then it can change us. Then we can live off it. When he was in prison in Tegel, Dietrich Bonhoeffer wrote about how he called up memories and how they brought him light and comfort in the loneliness of his cell. He kept the memory of meetings and experiences at church services or concerts in his heart and lived off them through that cold time. His ability to hold onto healing words and experiences gave an answer to Hoelderlin's complaint: "Woe is me, where can I get flowers and sunshine, if it is winter?" Bonhoeffer kept the flowers of his experience of God, so that they could also bloom in the barren desert of a brutal Nazi dungeon. He kept sunshine in his heart, so that the prison guards' grim coldness could not threaten him.

The Angel of Safekeeping does not want to lead you into a conservative position, or a flight from the present. It wants to show you how to protect and treasure what is precious in your experience, so that you can always marvel at it. This gives your life depth and richness. It also enables you to cope with unpleasant situations. You can keep going through barren patches without dying of thirst. People who cannot store things up always need fresh comfort, fresh food, fresh experiences in order to feel they are alive. The ability to preserve things keeps me alive, even when I am cut off from life, in times of deadness or defeat.

My wish for you is that the Angel of Safekeeping may enable you to live each moment intensely. May this Angel give you the power that Frederick had in the children's story, to gather the sun rays and the beauty of flowers into his heart in summer, so that he could live off them in winter.

THE ANGEL OF LEAVING

HUMAN BEINGS HAVE A DEEP LONGING to settle down in comfort, to make a home where they feel secure and protected. When we find somewhere pleasant, we want to pitch our tent and stay there forever. But we also know that in this world we cannot ever set up a permanent home. We have to keep moving on. We have to keep departing. We have to leave the home we have built where we feel comfortable and go on our way. Leaving means leaving something behind. We have to leave behind our old life. We cannot just go on with it. I cannot always stay where I am now.

As long as we are on the road we have to keep packing up our tents, in order to reach the new country. At first every departure causes anxiety. We have to leave our old familiar life behind. And while we are leaving something behind, we do not know what is before us. The unknown makes us afraid. At the same time, departure contains a promise, the promise of something new, somewhere we have never been or seen. If we do not keep moving on, our life will become paralyzed. If we do not keep changing, we will become old and stale. There are new possibilities for our life. But they can only take shape if we break away from old patterns.

We want to settle down where we feel comfortable and at home. The disciples on Mount Tabor wanted to build three huts, so that they could remain forever with the blissful experience of the transfiguration. But Jesus did not let them. The very next moment, the transfiguring light was obliterated by a dark cloud. They could not hang on to the experience; they had to leave and make their way down to the valley. There they would miss the light from the mountain.

Every deep religious experience tempts us to settle down with it forever, to cling to something we cannot hold. We cannot hold God. He is essentially the God of the exodus, the God of departure, the God who always tells us to leave. He speaks to Moses: "Why do you cry to me? Tell the people of Israel to depart" (Exod. 14:15). The people of Israel were afraid to leave. Of course they felt oppressed and enslaved in Egypt. But they came to terms with the foreign government. At least their flesh pots bellies were full. They wanted to leave, but at the same time they were afraid of departure. We frequently feel this same ambivalence. We are never content with our lives as they are. We too are also afraid to leave, to leave behind the familiar life and risk an inner and outer change. But we will only experience life if we are prepared to keep setting out on the road. Like the Israelites, we need an angel for this journey, who gives us the courage to depart, who holds his rod over the Red Sea of our fear, so that we can tread safely and confidently through our life's waters.

Today it is particularly difficult for the Angel of Leaving. The basic mood of our time is not to move on, as it was in the 1960s when there was a strong mood for change, created first by the Second Vatican Council in the Church and then in society by the student revolts. Today the mood is more one of resignation, self-pity, depression, and gloom. We prefer to moan that everything is so difficult and we can't do much about it.

This is why we need the Angel of Leaving today, to give us hope for our time. This Angel will enable us to depart for new shores, give us the courage to create new ways of being together, a new way of behaving toward creation, and a fresh political and economic imagination.

This also means that you must leave behind old preconceptions and worn out ideas. Removing internal blocks, opening up closed paths, giving up old customs and habits will enable you to set out for new ways of living and new stages of your life.

You will often hesitate because you do not know where the way leads. Then may the Angel of Leaving stand beside you and give you courage to go your own way.

THE ANGEL OF COMMUNITY

WE ALL LIVE in some sort of community—the community of the family, the community of the Church, our religious group, the community of our village or town. So what about the Angel of Community? The community in which we live is always at risk. It can break down if we do not communicate well with each other, if people just look out for themselves or hide behind their own prejudices. The Angel of Community wants to help you to experience the gift of true community.

A glance at our own history is illuminating. For the first Christians, the experience that community was possible between Jews and Gentiles, men and women, rich and poor, was proof that the kingdom of God had come. In his own person and with the Spirit he gave us, Jesus Christ had joined people as different as his apostles together in a community. For the early Christians the community was the place where they experienced God. It can be so again for us today. A community of people praying in a religious service or prayer group can have an intense experience of God. We feel that we are not alone, that God is with us. Jesus himself promised us: "Where two or three are gathered together in my name, there am I in the midst of them." Or if we are talking to a friend we might suddenly feel an intensity, a sense that heaven is opening to us and our heart is expanding. When this deep stillness comes over us, it is no accident that we say, "An angel is passing over." The Angel of Community is creating a new quality of being together.

We also have experienced that the community can fall apart. Then we try to sort things out between us, but we do not succeed. We rub each other the wrong way. When one conflict is settled, the next one breaks out. We feel powerless to pursue the ideal of community with which we began. We are disappointed, and we feel unable to grow together into a real living community. However, even this damaging experience can become a place where we find God. It can point you to the community of the angels where you are really at home, for there you can be yourself. There no one reproaches you. People do not project their own problems onto you. You need the Angel of Community to show you, in these dead-end situations, that there is still a deeper community, that you are involved in the community of angels. Then you feel that the ideal you have created of a Christian community cannot be fulfilled by your own efforts. In order to be able to live at all in this community, where there are so many conflicts and intrigues, so much human weakness and falsehood, you must have a deeper ground within you, a ground that is also beyond you. The community will never be able to fulfill your longing for home and security. It points you and your longing toward God.

A Hasidic story tells us that we can only live our own lives if we are prepared to share our lives with other people. A rabbi says, "Every human being is called to bring something to completion in the world.

The world needs each person. But there are people who continually sit indoors studying and do not go out of the house to talk to others. That is why they are called unkind. For if they conversed with others, they would bring some part of their tasks to completion. So being kind to yourself means not staying too long by yourself without going out to others. It means not being unkind through loneliness." There is a good sort of solitude, which makes us fit for community. But there is also a bad kind of solitude, which isolates us. We shut ourselves up in it and so do not contribute what the human community expects of us. We should make our own uniquely personal contribution to the community and thus, in our own way, make something of God's fullness appear in this world.

If you see the human community as a sign of the community God wants to give you, then you can enjoy it. Then you will always be grateful for the experience of being accepted. You know where you belong. There you can be yourself, just as you are. You do not have to prove yourself. You do not always have to fulfill expectations. You can let yourself slip. You can be weak for once. This, precisely, is a sign of Christian community, that we can also show our weaknesses and our wounds. Henri Nouwen once said that everything that we withhold from the community will deprive the community of liveliness. If we withhold our weaknesses, because we would prefer to hide them, then in an important way the community cannot flourish.

Community means sharing everything with one another, our strengths and our weaknesses. But there must always be room for our own secrets. There can be community only if each of us can also be ourselves. Because they want everything from their members, many Christian religious communities demand not only their members' money but all their thoughts and feelings as well. This oversteps the limit into the totalitarian. Community requires the breath and breadth of freedom. Solitude and community must be in healthy tension. If the community becomes absolute, we crowd each other so much that we can hardly breathe. The community will only be fruitful when each of us in the community can also go our own particular personal inner way. It will require us to go further along the way. It will show us our blind spots, so that we go the way of truth. On this way of truth we arrive at new insights about ourselves and our fellows.

May the Angel of Community continue to give you the experience of being with others that is so demanding and brings such happiness.

THE ANGEL OF CALM

To possess *nothing, to have every-thing,* describes the attitude of the wise in every religion in every age. Only those who do not set their hearts on anything created, those who can let go of things others hang on to, are really free. Calm was an important word for the medieval mystics. In particular, Meister Eckhart often speaks about calm. People are calm who have let go of their ego and given themselves up to God. They are those who have become peaceful at heart, because they have let themselves fall into the ground of the divine. For the mystics, calm means liberation from our own ego, letting go of all cares and anxieties about ourselves, so that God can

be born in our hearts, and we can recognize our true self in our inmost being, our genuine personal core. This calm is an attitude of inner freedom, inner tranquility, a sane distance from all the things that flood me from outside, threatening to 'occupy' and possess me. This attitude is not easy. But it can be practiced. In order to attain this calm, I have to let go of many things.

First I must let go of the world. So say the mystics. St. Anthony, the father of monasticism, left all his possessions in order to become free for life. We must stop hanging on to property, success, and recognition. If we hang on to earthly things we become dependent, and dependence goes against human dignity. Often enough we are dependent on our wellbeing, our habits, and on people. A story told by the early Fathers explains by a parable how we can only enjoy through letting go. A child sees many nuts in a glass jug; he reaches into it and tries to get as many as possible out of it, but his clenched fist will not fit through the jug's narrow neck. First he has to let go of the nuts. Then he can take them out one by one to enjoy.

Letting go is not an ascetic performance that we must force upon ourselves. Rather, it comes from a longing for inner freedom and the feeling that our lives can only really be fruitful if we are free and independent. If we are no longer dependent on what others think and expect of us, if we are no longer dependent on the support and recognition of others, then we get into touch with our real self.

But calm detachment also means letting go of myself. I must not cling on to myself, my cares, my fears, and my feelings of depression. Many people cling on to their injuries. They cannot let go of them. They use them to accuse people who have hurt them. In the end this is a refusal of life. We must also let go of our injuries and sicknesses. You need the Angel of Calm to teach you the art of letting go of yourself and your past, to show you how to distance yourself from yourself, stand back, and look at your life from a different point of view, from a position beyond your own self.

If you are calm in this way you can react calmly to the sensationalist reports in the media. You can reply calmly to criticism and rejection. Every criticism does not send you into a panic. You do not feel threatened. You are not afraid that the ground will be swept from under your feet. You have achieved some distance from all inner and outer disturbance. You know you are supported by the Angel of Calm, who tells you: "There is more than the opinion that others have of you. There is more than success and image. Let yourself go in God. There you will find firm ground on which to stand. From there you can look calmly at everything pouring in on you from outside."

If you are detached from yourself, you can react in a calm, detached way to bad news. Composure is the expression of an inner discipline. Even though composed people are shaken inside, they do not show their dismay. They restrain their behavior and control themselves. Calmness does not mean self-control. Calm people do not need to restrain their behavior; they have a different point of view because they are not inwardly hit by the bad news. Because they are detached from themselves and their idea of how their life should go, nothing throws them off course easily. The Angel of Calm helps them to regard everything they hear from the Angel's own distance. This gives them inner freedom and space.

Many people get carried away in a heated discussion. They say their conscience requires them to stand for the truth. The Angel of Calm shows you that in such a discussion, truth does not lie in the rightness of the words or the arguments, but somewhere else, on a different level. Truth means harmony, agreement with reality. What we hold as absolutely true is often only the expression of our own projections. We make images of the truth for ourselves, images of God. Truth itself is incomprehensible. It cannot be defined. If we know about the deepest truth, we go calmly into the discussion, not resignedly, because we cannot know the truth. We know that our knowledge is always relative, that there can always be different points of view, that the truth will probably lie somewhere between the opinions of the disputing parties.

Against the reasoning that insists it has the monopoly onf rightness, the philosopher Martin Heidegger suggested a calm detachment and an openness to mystery: "You have to think constantly from the heart in order for both of these to flourish."

My wish for you is that the Angel of Calm may help you not to think too much with your head but also to listen with your heart.

THE ANGEL OF PASSION

THE ANGEL OF PASSION seems to contradict the Angel of Calm, but we need many angels to make our lives prosper. The Angel of Passion challenges us to live with all our hearts, not just to exist keep ourselves on the back burner. When people are no longer capable of great passion, their lives become boring and insipid. They lose the taste for life. This is definitely not what

Jesus wanted for us; he told us to be salt for the earth, to season this world with our zest. Passions are natural, compelling forces in human beings, which drive them to live to the fullest and should direct them finally to God. The Angel of Passion should teach us the art of deploying these driving forces to make them forces for life. We should not be ruled by them, but we can use them for our life's own purposes. We should not become driven people, who allow ourselves to be driven, but people whose passion drives them to serve life and to create life in its many forms.

People who can get passionately involved in something can fight passionately for life. Their spirituality will also be passionate. A Hasidic story points toward this. "A Hasid once complained to Rabbi Wolf about some people who spent all night playing cards. 'That's good,' said the Zaddik. 'Like all people they want to serve God and do not know how. But now they are learning to keep awake and stick to a task. If they seek perfection, all they need to do is change the task — and then what great servants of God they will be!"

The old monks thought a great deal about the passions. Evagrius Ponticus (who died in 399) counted nine passions that monks must struggle with. For him the passions were positive forces. It is not a question of suppressing them, but of integrating them into our lives. The passions should serve us, rather than us our serving them. Apatheia, which is the goal of the struggle with the passions, does not mean a passionless condition but freedom from being pathologically ensnared by passion. It means integration of the passions in everything I do and think, a state in which the passions no longer rule me but are at my disposal as power, as virtus, as virtue, which helps make me alive.

Passions are value-free. Whether they are good or bad depends on how I act with them. Anger is a positive power, which can enable me to separate myself from something and, free myself from the power of others. But it can also consume me, if I allow myself to be controlled by it. Sexuality can bring me to life, but it can also take me over. Fullness of living does not come from repressing or giving full rein to the passions, but from awareness in of the way we handle them. Those who live without passion lack bite, lack force, lack fullness of life. Many

Christians have killed off their passions by sheer striving for correctto act correctlyness. They have become boring. They are no longer the salt of the earth, no longer seasoning for our world, but insipid and dull. Jesus sided passionately with the poor and the oppressed. He spoke passionately of the merciful Father, and fought passionately against the hardheartedness of the Pharisees, who had darkened God's image by their petty narrow observances of the law.

The word 'passion' comes from the Latin root *patiens*, meaning to suffer, just as *Leidenschaft*, the German word for passion, comes from *leiden*, meaning to suffer. This word *Lleiden* formerly meant to go, travel, or journey. If you go somewhere you experience, you undergo something. Thus the word *leiden* gradually acquired the meaning of putting up with, bearing pain. So passion has to do with experience. If you suppress it, you lose experience. If you go with it, you experience the new, the unimagined. But just as every journey can be arduous, so can the experience of passion. Life is always a balancing act. A passion can all too easily become stronger than is good for us. Then we do not live our own life with passion, but passion controls us. May the Angel of Passion accompany you in your balancing act, so that you can become a really genuinely passionate person, a person who engages passionately with others, and passionately fights for the possibility of a life that is worthy of humanity for everyone on this earth.

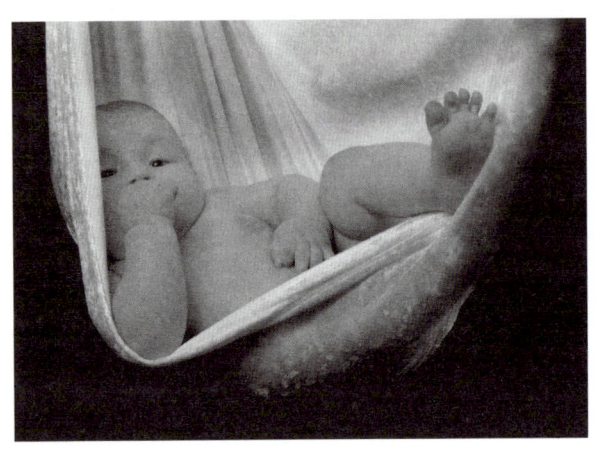

THE ANGEL
OF TRUTHFULNESS

WE CALL PEOPLE TRUTHFUL when they are genuine and consistent. Jesus said of Nathanael: "Here comes a genuine Israelite, in whom there is no guile" (John 1:47). Truthful people do not live by calculation but by their own inner truth. They are free of intrigue, diplomacy, and consideration of how best to sell themselves to others. They live in harmony with themselves. They are genuine. They say what they think. They behave as they feel in their hearts. With such people you always know where you are. They do not hide their thoughts and feelings. They are not afraid to be known. They behave as they are, because they stand by everything that is in them. They hide nothing, because they have nothing to hide, because they are as they should be.

A truthful person is always free, for only truth can make us free. Today there are so many people who depart from their own truth. They are afraid to face the truth of their own hearts. They get into a panic when for once if they have to be quiet even for a moment. For then something they find unpleasant might well up in them. So they have to keep busy, simply in order to keep away from their own truth. They are always rushing and frantic. The worst thing that can happen to them is a moment when nothing is happening, when their own truth might come to light. If you evade your own truth you need a lot of energy to hide it from others. You are always wondering what other people are thinking about you. You rack your brain thinking about what you should say so that you sound all right to others, so that they do not start wondering about your psyche, your repressed drives, your complexes. You anxiously analyze every word in case it might suggest a neurotic complex or a repressed shadow.

The Greek word for truth is aletheia, which means when things are not hidden. The veil is drawn back, and we see what actually, really is. Truthful people hide nothing; their true self is out in the open. The Angel of Truthfulness wants to keep opening your eyes to your true reality. The Angel takes away the veil that lies over everything. It removes the glasses with which you look at everything. Perhaps you are wearing dark glasses, which falsify everything. You only see the negative side. Or perhaps you are wearing rose-colored tinted spectacles. You are not willing to see people and as they are with their problems. You imagine things so that you can live more comfortably. The Angel of Truthfulness takes away all your glasses. The Angel shows you the reality. "When God sends his angel to the soul, it becomes truly knowing," writes Meister Eckhart.

A truthful person forces us to face the truth of our own heart. In the company of a truthful person we can hide nothing from ourselves. We find the courage to show our own truth. When Jesus spoke, the unclean spirits and troubled thoughts that plague people and harm them with poisonous feelings could no longer be hidden. They were dragged out into the light by the word of Jesus. This is how Mark describes it: When Jesus preached for the first time in the synagogue, the unclean spirit in a man cried out. It felt that it could no longer hide behind critical and ironical expressions. It had to come out into the truth. The unclean spirit had to go out of the man; it had to set him free (cf. Mark 1:23ff). Jesus's truthfulness frees people from unclean spirits, which alter and falsify the truth. Jesus heals them, so that they become genuinely truthful people.

I wish you the Angel of Truthfulness, so that you can be wholly as you are in the depths of your being, so that you can free the people around you to the truth. Truth also means that the object and our knowledge of it coincide; the thing corresponds to our idea of it. They agree. My wish for you is that you may be wholly in agreement with yourself and the reality of your life.

THE ANGEL OF GRATITUDE

WE LACK GRATITUDE TODAY. We are
making make limitless demands.
We easily get the impression that we
have been sold short. So we want more and
more. In some ways we have become insa-
tiable and so are no longer capable of real
enjoyment. The French philosopher Pascal
Bruckner describes people today as giant
babies with unbounded demands on society.

We can never get enough, and it is always other people's fault when things go wrong. Often we feel that we are not given what we absolutely must have to live our lives.

The Angel of Gratitude would like to bring a new taste into your life. It She would like to teach you to look at everything with new eyes, grateful eyes. Then you can be thankful for the new day, that you have your health and can get up and see the sun rise. You are become grateful for the breath that is in your body. You are grateful for nature's good gifts, which you can enjoy for at breakfast. You are aware. Gratitude opens your heart and brings in joy. You are not obsessed with the things that might annoy you. You do not begin the morning grumbling about the weather. You are not infuriated when the milk pot boils over. At times we make our lives difficult because we see only the negative side. And the more we see the negative, the more our experience confirms it. A pessimistic view of things attracts misfortune.

The word 'thank' comes from 'think.' The Angel of Gratitude would like to teach you to think accurately and carefully. When you begin to think, you will recognize thankfully all that has been given to you. You will be grateful that your parents have given you your life. You will not only be grateful for the positive roots your parents gave you, but also for the wounds and injuries you have received from them, because they have also made you who you now are. Without these wounds you might have become self-centered and insensitive. You might not have come to see the needs of people around you. The Angel of Gratitude wants to open your eyes to the fact that an angel of God has accompanied you all through your life, a guardian angel has protected you from misfortunes, and your guardian angel has transformed even your injuries into precious treasure. The Angel of Gratitude gives you new eyes to behold the beauty of creation, to enjoy the beauty of meadows and forests, mountains and valleys, oceans, rivers, and lakes.

New eyes to marvel at the grace of a gazelle and the delicacy of a deer. You will no longer walk through creation numb, but mindfully and filled with gratitude. You will realize in creation that you are touched by the loving God who wants to demonstrate how extravagantly which He cares for you.

When you look at your life with gratitude, you accept what has happened. You stop rebelling against yourself and your fate. You know that every day an angel comes into your life anew, to protect you from harm and give you its loving and healing company. Try to go through the coming week with the Angel of Gratitude. You will see everything in a new light, and your life will acquire a new taste.

You can also ask your Angel of Gratitude to teach you to be grateful for the people you live with. We often pray for the people who are important to us only if we want to change them or if we want God to help, heal, or comfort them. Often our prayer for others is a prayer against them. We would like them to become the way we want them to be. But iIf we say thank you for another person, then we accept them unconditionally as they are. We do not want to change them. They are valuable, just as they are. People notice when we give thanks for them. Our gratitude sends out a positive affirmation, in which they feel themselves accepted as they are. A clergyman once told the story of a married couple who had prayed for many years for the wife's alcoholic father, that he would be able to get free of his alcohol addiction. They offered their petition in countless prayer groups, but nothing happened. Then they gained the courage to be grateful for their father, just for his being alive, for his being who he was. Only then did they empower him to change. Because he no longer felt unconsciously pressured by them to change, he was able to change. Because he felt he was unconditionally accepted, he no longer needed alcohol. Therefore, ask your Angel of Gratitude for the miracle that through your gratitude, others may feel unconditionally loved, and in this love become whole and healed.

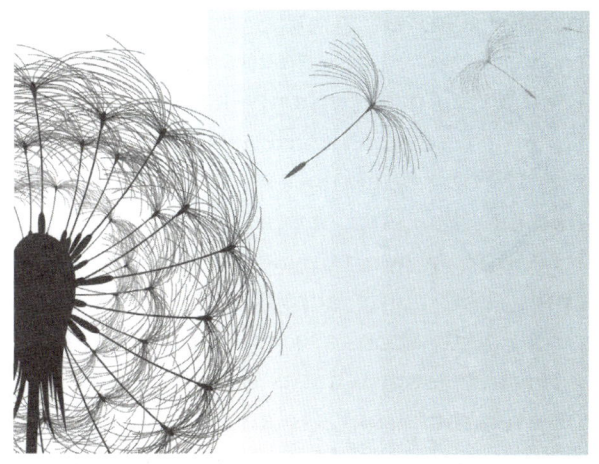

THE ANGEL
OF RENUNCIATION

THINGS ARE DIFFICULT nowadays for the Angel of Renunciation. Many people associate the word 'renunciation' with gloomy asceticism. After all, God wants us to live life to the full. Why then renounce things? Today life is all about consuming and finding pleasure. Sure, there are enough examples of people who are giving up so much that they've become unbearable. But does renunciation necessarily lead to an attitude of resentment? Renunciation means to give up my claim to something that is due me. The goal of renunciation is inner freedom. When you need to have everything you come across, you are totally dependent. You are not free. You are governed from what is outside yourself.

Renunciation is an expression of inner freedom. If I can give up something I enjoy, I am inwardly free. Renunciation can also be a training in inner freedom. If, for example, I give up alcohol and meat for Lent, this can be a training in freedom. I test whether for six weeks I am able to give up television, alcohol, smoking, meat, or perhaps even coffee. If I succeed, I feel good. I have the feeling that I am no longer a slave to my habits, that I do not have to have alcohol to stimulate me. This gives me a feeling of inner freedom. It contributes to my self-respect. If I feel I just have to drink coffee when I am tired, I become dependent upon it. Ultimately this disturbs me.

It takes away my dignity as a person in control of myself. I feel I can no longer determine how I behave; I am dominated by my needs.

I was once invited to take part in a television program with a pleasure researcher and a sex researcher. The program was called *Renunciation, Enjoyment, or Both?* I, a monk, was also asked about my take on enjoyment and renunciation. In the end, all three of us agreed that there can be no enjoyment without renunciation. If you want only to enjoy, you will not succeed. I can happily enjoy one or even two slices of cake. But by at least the fourth slice I am no longer enjoying it; I am just cramming it in. Today we have often become incapable of enjoyment, because we are no longer able to give things up. It used to be the other way round. In earlier centuries it was made hard for Christians to enjoy life because the focus was on living ascetically. There was suspicion of enjoyment. This was just as one-sided a view as the modern idea that we need to have everything. When greedy, we cannot enjoy. My wish for you is that the Angel of Renunciation may lead you to inner freedom. I hope it will make you able really to enjoy what you experience, to really get involved in what you are doing, to feel with all your senses what you are eating and what you are drinking. You will find that the Angel of Renunciation is also an angel of joy and enjoyment, who will do you good. When you give up your claim to what you are entitled to — food, drink, television, and the like — you gain yourself. You take your life into your own hands. The Angel of Renunciation would like to teach you the art of living your own life, freely disposing of yourself, so that your life is a pleasure to you.

THE ANGEL OF RISK

OFTEN IT IS THOUGHT that the most important thing in life is not to be conspicuous or make a mistake. Then your career will not be threatened. You will not be criticized in your group. Your life will be a success. In reality, this fear of taking risks is a hindrance to life. If you are determined not to make a single mistake, you will do everything wrong.

Because you dare nothing and risk nothing, nothing new can happen. In business and in politics, in society and in church, no one seems willing to take risks anymore. For this would lay them open to attack—things might go wrong, and that would be a catastrophe. They would no longer sit softly cushioned but have to stand up and face themselves and their mistakes. Many are afraid they would not survive this. They are so set upon the respect and recognition of others that they no longer trust their own instincts, and dare not risking anything.

Psychology tells us that fear of taking risks is connected with the lack of a father, so common in our society. Traditionally, the father is the one who gives us backbone, gives us courage to dare something or take a risk. If we do not have this positive experience of a father, our backbone will need support. So we lean upon an ideology or on what is regarded as the norm. We play it safe. We don't experiment. We do everything the same old way. We do not allow ourselves to think anything new, so we do not do anything different. There is no guarantee that the new thing will be successful. So we don't do it. Our life is marked by lack of imagination and lack of the courage to risk anything. The word 'risk' comes from Italian and means danger and daring. Many claim that life should go by without danger. You have to insure yourself against all dangers so that nothing can happen to you. But the more you insure yourself, the more insecure you become. Gradually you no longer trust yourself. Everything has to be insured. We dare nothing without comprehensive security. This leads to greater and greater paralysis. Only if we take risks, if we dare to make mistakes, can we get out of this blind alley.

My wish for you is that the Angel of Risk may give you courage to be daring in your life and to risk new actions for the benefit of yourself and the people around you. May the Angel of Risk strengthen your backbone and keep your back free, so that you are free to risk yourself and trust your inmost impulses, without constantly needing insurance and support. The world will be grateful to you if you dare to do something new, if you do not first ask anyone and everyone for permission to put your ideas into practice. We experience every day that the old ideas will not do. No one dares follow a new course in the matter of unemployment. We prefer to entrench ourselves in the commonplace or to pass the blame on to others. Everyone waits for someone else to take a false step. Then we can criticize them. But no one dares take the first step. We keep marching on the same spot. We wait for others to make mistakes instead of risking a mistake ourselves. My wish for you is that the Angel of Risk should give you the strength and freedom to dare making mistakes and to open up new ways for yourself and humanity. Only when you trust the Angel of Risk can you bring something new into the world, and then through you people can discover new possibilities.

THE ANGEL OF CONFIDENCE

WE HAVE GOTTEN so used to prophets of doom constantly alarming us with their visions of an apocalyptic future, we badly need the Angel of Confidence. Prophecies announcing the end of the world are rampant . Of course no one can guarantee that our world will remain in balance for a long time to come and survive human follies. Yet the urge to prophesy the end of the world says more about the psyche of prophets than about the reality of our world. When we experience our own lives as a catastrophe and unconsciously nurture the wish that this ruined life may end, we project our own situation onto the world and hope that the world will end soon, too. This inner destructiveness then flows into a language of fire and brimstone. Because fear of the future is widespread today, these false prophets often meet a receptive audience and in the process gain power over many anxious people.

The Angel of Confidence gives us hope and trust in the future. We are empowered to follow what is happening with our eyes, to see how God guides and leads everything, how God sends out his angels, not to abandon this world to evil but to turn everything to good. In this confidence I do not let myself be shaken by pessimistic forecasts. I do not put on rose-colored glasses in order to distort reality. I do not have any illusions about the state of the world. I recognize how it is. Nevertheless, I am confident. I know that this world is in the hands of God and his angels, that human beings have no ultimate power over it. This confidence sees more than what is immediately in sight. It sees more than the problems with which newspaper headlines bombard us. In addition to the external, it sees the inmost reality of things. With the world, this confidence sees God's angels, who accompany us and keep their guarding hand over our land and our earth.

The Angel of Confidence has long been with those who pray the psalms: "The Angel of the Lord encamps around those who fear him, and delivers them." And in Psalm 91:11f: "For he will give his angels charge of you to guard you in all your ways. In their hands they will bear you up, lest you dash your foot against a stone."

Marie Luise Kaschnitz, author of Circe's Mountain, illustrates this confidence with the story about the ship owner Giovanni di Mata. He gave all his gold to the corsairs

(for centuries the predominant pirates off
the North African Coast) to buy the freedom of prisoners they had taken. As he was
about to put out to sea with the freed prisoners, the robbers demanded more money.
Because he could not meet their demands,
they smashed his mast and helm and ripped
his sails to shreds. Nevertheless, Giovanni
di Mata gave the signal to set out. To the
corsairs' astonishment, even without mast,
sails, and helm, the ship slowly began to
move and reached the open sea.

Likewise, the confident are given the
knowledge that an angel protects us and
shields us, that it even carries us in its

hands, so that we can tread safely among lions and vipers. The confident believe an angel looks after them, so that nothing bad can harm them.

They do not walk blindly through the world. They see when danger looms. But they know they are accompanied by their angel. They know they are protected and supported. They know they are not just a number, at the mercy of fate, but that an angel goes with them, takes care of them, and frees them from all their fears.

THE ANGEL OF SOLITUDE

TODAY MANY OF US ARE AFRAID of being alone. When we are alone, we do not feel like ourselves. We need other people around us all the time just to feel alive. But solitude can be a blessing. Without solitude, there can be no real relationship with God and no genuine self-knowledge. Many people confuse solitude with being abandoned and with loneliness and isolation, but solitude is an essential part of every spiritual journey. All the great religious founders went through a time in the wilderness away from others. Jesus endured solitude when he fasted for forty days in the wilderness. There he confronted his own reality and found God his Father in a new way.

I wish the Angel of Solitude for you. I hope it will lead you into a fruitful solitude, where you can get to know yourself as you really are; where there's no point in making yourself interesting to others, and you must confront your own nakedness. When you gather the courage to be alone, you will discover how delightful it can be to be completely by yourself — no need to show off or prove anything, no need to justify yourself. Then perhaps you will experience being completely at one with yourself.

The word 'alone' says this — you are all-one. All-one in three ways. First, you are wholly at one with yourself. The ancient Greeks longed for oneness. They felt torn between diverse desires and needs. Today we understand this longing for oneness anew. The multiplicity of our desires and possibilities pulls us here and there. How among all the potential parts within me can I find my own oneness, the clasp that holds everything together?

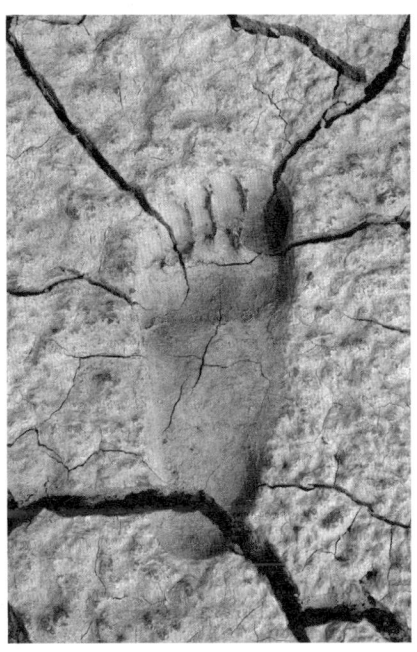

The second meaning of alone or all-one refers to all humanity. It means being one with all and everyone, to feel profoundly connected with all human beings in solidarity. The more I face my own solitude, the deeper I feel my connection with other people. The early monks experienced this when they consciously chose solitude. They withdrew from people in order to become one with them at a deeper level. Evagrius Ponticus, one of the most important writers among the monks, expresses it thus: "A monk is a human being who has cut himself off from everything and therefore feels connected with everything. A monk knows he is one with all human beings, because he keeps finding himself in every human being." In my loneliness I discover my foundation, the ground of my being, wherein I find myself deeply connected with all people. There I sense that nothing human is alien to me, that in my inmost self I am united with everybody else.

The third meaning of being alone has to do with the all of the universe. The philosopher Friedrich Nietzsche says: "He who knows ultimate solitude knows the ultimate things." In being alone I become one with all of creation, with the final truth, with the very source of all being. This experience of being alone is an essential part of being human. Therefore, the writer Fyodor Dostoyevsky says: "Being alone from time to time is more necessary for a common human being than eating and drinking." In solitude I become aware of the essence of my humanity; I understand that I take part in everything, in the entire universe, and ultimately in the One who is all in all. If the Angel of Solitude leads you into this fundamental experience of your humanity, then you lose all fear of loneliness and of being left alone. Then you feel that there, where you are alone, you are one with all. Then you experience your solitude not as being lonely but as being home. But home you can only be where mystery dwells.

Where the Angel of Solitude leads, into the ultimate mystery that rules this world, you are never alone. There you are really at home. This mystery, which embraces all, gives you a home no one can take from you.

THE ANGEL
OF SISTERHOOD

THE BIBLE REPEATEDLY SPEAKS of 'philadelphia', of brotherly and sisterly love. The early Christians experienced it as great bliss that not only were their physical siblings brothers and sisters, but the whole community became a community of brothers and sisters. May the Angel of Sisterhood and Brotherhood show you how many brothers and sisters you gain if you yourself approach people as brothers and sisters.

Indeed, this was the fundamental experience of the first Christians, that all members of these early communities became brothers and sisters. The reason for this was that they all had the same Father. Because we may all pray together to our Father in heaven, we are all brothers and sisters in his sight and under him. Jesus calls anyone who does God's will "brother and sister" (Mark 3:35). When we draw close to this example, gather round Jesus, and are prepared like him to do the Father's will, then we become brothers and sisters in Christ. Then a new family arises, in which all have equal rights. Jesus forbids the disciples to call themselves Rabbi. "For only one is your master, but all of you are brothers" (Matt. 23:8). The Angel of Sisterhood can show us that we all have equal rights, that none of us should put ourselves above others. For it's often that we place ourselves above others, not only by our social rank, but even more so by our prejudice. We feel we are better than others; we raise ourselves above them. We concentrate on their negative sides, and do not even notice how we project our own weaknesses onto them. It is a widely spread mechanism by which we project our faults onto others, and thus rate ourselves above them. This way we keep apart from others and so protect ourselves from having to look our own truth in the eye.

Once we've come to know ourselves we stop trying to see our own faults in others. But then we become truly brother or sister to others, for we see ourselves in them.

Having a sister is different from having a brother. I am lucky in my family because

I have three sisters and three brothers. There is my eldest sister, who often took our mother's place when we were children.

She is like the Angel of Sisterhood, who looks after us like a mother. She is not a big mother who swallows us, but she gives sisterly loving care. She does not stand over us but sits beside us. She is tender and understanding. She discovers needs that a mother cannot fulfill. Then there are sisters of the same age, companions for the way. With brothers you stay together through thick and thin. With sisters you have intense conversations and you strike chords in yourself that with brothers would remain mute. Then there are younger sisters. It is not for nothing that we often give them *angelic* names. The Angel of Sisterhood brings me into contact with my anima, my emotional nature and my spirituality. Angels have always stood in a sisterly relation to our souls. Helmut Hark, a Protestant priest and therapist, speaks of the erotic relationship between our soul and the angel who is our spiritual companion. If we look at angels in an art book we often discover their erotic aura. They awaken passion in our soul, which is otherwise only stirred by a lover. The Angels' erotic power has a healing effect on us.

The experience of a sister can bring us into touch with our inner angel. The sister herself can become an angel, who brings to sound the tender strings of our soul, who brings the spiritual energies in us to life and heals our broken heart. Therefore I wish you may meet many Angels of Sisterhood, and I wish that you yourself may become a stimulating and enlivening Angel of Sisterhood.

THE ANGEL
OF SELF–SURRENDER

SELF-SURRENDER — that may at first sound rather passive and resigned. People who do not succeed in actively shaping and controlling their lives simply surrender themselves to fate. They give up on themselves. However, this is not the direction the Angel of Self-Surrender would want to lead us. Self-surrender can mean something quite different. First of all, self-surrender has to do with surrendering ourselves to something. When we surrender ourselves to life, we give ourselves to life and its dynamic. We do not hold ourselves back. We do not clench up within ourselves but surrender to the flow of life. Then something can come alive and blossom in us.

Self-surrender is the opposite of holding onto ourselves. Some of us cling to our self-image, or we cling to our habits or possessions, our name, or our success. The Angel of Self-Surrender would like to lead you into the art of letting yourself go, surrendering yourself to life, and ultimately to God. I can surrender myself only if I trust that I am not surrendering to an arbitrary fate but to an angel, who wants the best for me. When you surrender to your angel, you become free of the unnecessary concerns that plague us today. Then your life stops revolving around yourself and your health, recognition, and success. This attitude of self-surrender consists not only of trust but of great inner freedom. When I do not have to do everything myself, when I simply surrender myself to God, trusting that he will take care of me, I become free of all self-absorption and self-centeredness.

The Angel of Self-Surrender would also like to help you trust enough to surrender yourself to another person. Many friendships and marriages today fail because the partners hang on to themselves, because they are afraid of self-surrender. They fear that they will lose their freedom, the other person will dominate them, and they will become victims of his or her whims or even ill will. But no relationship can succeed without this self-surrender. We are bound to fail when as friends and partners we anxiously try to control our emotions, words, and actions, so as not to give ourselves over to the other. Then trust cannot grow; the other person cannot show that he or she means well by us and will not abuse our trust. Self-surrender does not mean giving up on yourself. You can only surrender yourself when you are in touch with yourself, if you know who you are. But at the same time there is always a risk in this self-surrender. We lose the security of holding onto ourselves when we surrender ourselves to another person. This is beneficial only if I know that the other has my best interests at heart and is not a devil but an angel who will catch hold of me and carry me safely.

We may often think that we have to do everything ourselves. We work hard in order to get on and realize our ideals. We struggle to do good. But at some time or another we reach the point when we realize that we cannot get everything we want. We have so many good intentions, but we cannot fulfill them all. Again and again we are confronted with our own inadequate reality. This is the time to open up and surrender to the angel God sends to make our lives succeed. It is not resignation but freedom. I realize I do not have to achieve everything I wanted to; that was simply my own ambition and by no means the will of God. When I stand before God in meditation and hold out my empty hands to him, I feel the freedom that comes from self-surrender. I let myself rely on God. I know that God supports me, that in God's kind hands I can be simply as I am. This is the core of belief of Christians: the experience of the freedom that Christ brings (cf. Gal. 5:1).

THE ANGEL OF WARMTH

SOME PEOPLE, WE SAY, RADIATE warmth. We feel good when we are with them. Other people emit cold. When we are near such a person we freeze up even in summer. The Angel of Warmth energizes you to radiate warmth, so that people near you feel secure and loved. This angel helps you to keep finding people who become Angels of Warmth for you. When you are with them your frozen feelings thaw out — you can warm yourself in their company when this cold world has made you shiver. Many of us find today's world cold. It is rare that we feel comfortable enough to take off our protective gear when we are with others. We are afraid of others' cold gaze. We all may at some point barricade ourselves behind a wall of cold. Angels of Warmth benefit us. They make encounter and intimacy possible. They create an atmosphere in which we feel fine; we feel at home.

The question is what can you do that allows the Angel of Warmth to enable you to warm up the people around you. For me it is vital to keep putting myself in the warmth of God's love, so that my heart warms up for others. Henri Nouwen sees the spiritual life as tending an inner fire, which burns in all of us. Nouwen thinks many people today are burnt out, because they have opened the door of their stove too wide to the outside world, so they cannot keep up their glowing heat. It will quickly turn to burnt-out ashes. For me, too, spiritual life means tending the inner fire. It helps me when I am meditating to fold my arms and imagine that I am now closing the door of my stove, so that now the fire of God's love can glow through everything in me and transform it. Then I feel a pleasant warmth inside me, and I know that the fire of God's love extends to all. Then my ability to show warmth to others doesn't rely on my resolve. When I tend my inner fire through prayer, I become warm inside, and this warmth will be enough for all the people I meet today.

You cannot fake a warm glow. You cannot plan it in advance. When I look at the Gothic paintings of angels, especially Fra Angelico's angels, they warm my heart. They are angels who radiate warmth. In them there is nothing gloomy, nothing cold, nothing hostile. What the great medieval physician Paracelsus once said about angels is true: "You should know: an angel is the human being without the mortal share."

Because angels lack the mortal, the destructive and pathological, we can warm up in their presence without burning. See how good this warmth feels when you behold an angel. And you will find that warmth will glow from you as well. Be grateful for this. The warmth that radiates from you can warm others without taking away from the warmth you need. It warms us all because it is fed by the source of divine warmth, because it constantly blazes up with the fire of divine love.

The Angel of Warmth will energize you so that it will be easy for you to get warm with others. Warmth will radiate back and forth, and it will not take away from you.

On the contrary, the warmth that radiates between you will grow stronger. It creates an atmosphere that others will sense as well. When I am with a group of people I sense immediately whether a cold atmosphere dominates, whether one has to be careful of every word. Similarly, we sense where there is a warm atmosphere, an atmosphere of good will and friendliness. Then each word does not have to be weighed. There I can be as I am. There I am accepted wholly. My wish for you is that you always feel the Angel of Warmth around you and that you yourself may become an Angel of Warmth for others, someone who radiates a warmth that warms the heart of another.

THE ANGEL OF COURAGE

THE ENGLISH 'MOOD' is related to the old Germanic word *muot* which meant "to strive or violently long for something, to yearn." It corresponds to the Greek word *thymos*, which denotes the emotional side of the soul. From the sixteenth century onward, the German word *Mut* has increasingly acquired the meaning of bravery. Bravery is one of the four cardinal virtues. It means being unafraid in the face of danger. According to the ethicist Klaus Demmer, it arises from good spirits and demands willingness to make sacrifices, the power to carry things through and the will to assert oneself. Courage and bravery are required not only of soldiers but of everyone. We all need courage to live our lives, lives we were destined to from the start. All too easily we adapt to others, take on their ideas, and do not swim against the current. Today a liberalism prevails that permits everything. But at the same time we observe a great uniformity. The media establishes the norms of how to behave, how to think, how to dress, and what to do. It requires great courage to be different, to be what is right and fitting for ourselves.

You need the Angel of Courage when your fellow workers are demolishing a colleague. It requires courage not to join in the carping, when you say it might be better to speak to her instead; or when you break off the conversation, remarking that all this could be seen in another light. You may be misunderstood. Perhaps you will be accused of being a Pharisee. The others have made clear that they find the person being discussed quite impossible. People won't shift gears easily. If you have the courage to interrupt gossip about someone else, the scandalmongers feel embarrassed and may want to justify themselves by turning on you. Then you need courage to assert your opinion, even when others try to exclude you and accuse you of being very ready to gossip about other people yourself.

May the Angel of Courage stand at your side when you have to make decisions — decisions about your career and your life. Marriage, a life-long commitment to another person, is just one of these choices. Every decision binds us, at least for the time being, and we are very much afraid of this commitment. In the moment before important decisions, ask the Angel of Courage to help you. You can never have a guarantee that your decision is perfect.

There is never one absolutely right path to take. Nevertheless, when we come to a crossroads we have to decide which way to go. To move on we have to choose one way or another. And every way eventually leads to a narrow pass, through which we must travel if our lives are to expand. Jesus tells us to go through the narrow gate along the narrow road (cf. Matt. 7:13f). The broad road is the road traveled by all. But you have to find your own way. It is not enough to take your direction from others. You must listen carefully to discover your own path. Then you must bravely decide to walk this path, even when on the way you feel very lonely. Only your very own way will lead you to personal growth and truthful living.

The Angel of Courage can help you to deal with what is requested of you right now. This might be a conversation in your family to sort things out. It might be facing a problem at work that everyone else has put off. It might be a visit you have long postponed and prefer to avoid. It may be a letter you finally want to write to clarify a relationship or sort out a misunderstanding. There are so many situations in your everyday life when you need the Angel of Courage, so that you can do what is appropriate and so that you can do it now.

THE ANGEL OF PATIENCE

WAITING PATIENTLY IS out of fashion
nowadays.
Blessed are those who wait.
The globe whistles past them.
The sharpest bit of the world
doesn't break their gaze
from the promised course.
So writes the poet Ulla Hahn. The Angel
of Patience illustrates this beatitude, that

the Kingdom of Heaven belongs to the patient.

The word 'patience' comes from the Latin word *patiens*, meaning suffering. In the New Testament the Greek word used for patience, *hypomene*, actually means to be under or to stay under, to endure, or to hold out. Sometimes patience is regarded too passively, as if it were a matter simply of accepting things as they are. In the early Church, the meaning of patience was closer to endurance, steadfastness through the hardships threatening Christians from the outside world. In his Letter to the Romans (5:3) the apostle Paul says: "Suffering produces endurance, endurance produces character, and character produces hope." And in his Letter to the Colossians (1:11) he prays: "May you be strengthened with all power, according to his glorious might, for all endurance and patience with joy." Here hypomene means steadfast endurance, as needed in battle when a man must defend the position in which he finds himself against all enemy attacks. This quality of the power to hold out against external attacks is definitely relevant to our lives today. Here patience is not passive suffering but active endurance and holding out. It is *enduring resistance*. Paul relates it also to forbearance, in ancient Greek: *makrothymia*. For him this is a fruit of the Spirit (cf. Gal. 5:22). The Greek word means that you have great courage, great character, and a big heart, all of which make you able to wait. In the course of history the word patience has taken on all these meanings: steadfastness, endurance, and also the ability to wait and forbear, watching patiently until a solution is found.

May the Angel of Patience help you to wait. This is not an obvious quality today. We want solutions right away, yet it may take a long time for a flower to bloom. We need patience for our own development. We cannot change ourselves all at once. Transformation happens slowly and sometimes unnoticeably. Bible images still speak

to us today. Jesus gave us the parable of the seed that grows by itself (cf. Mark 4:26-9). James also takes farmers as an example in his letter: "Behold the farmer waits for the precious fruit of the earth, being patient over it until it receives the early and the late rain. You also be patient" (James. 5:7f). Often we want instant success as soon as we have begun something. In therapy we want instant progress, and in spiritual counseling we want instant results. The desire to control our success leads us to overlook what is slowly ripening within us. We urgently need the Angel of Patience to give our inner processes time to develop. Growth requires time. What shoots up fast also withers fast.

Patience does not mean refusing to consider everything that can be changed and should be changed. But you should also be patient with yourself and with any situation that cannot be changed and demands calmness. May the Angel of Patience stand by you, when you have to bear something hard or endure a painful situation. Marriage problems or conflicts at work cannot always be solved quickly or at all. There too we need patient endurance. But patience does not mean coming to terms with conflict permanently or accepting an uneasy compromise. Patience includes the power to work toward change and transformation. Time plays an important part in patience. We give ourselves and other people time for something to change.

We need patience when we are ill. We cannot get over it all at once. Today the power simply to endure something is becoming more rare. To hold out patiently, to endure, to keep going, is a virtue that is not often asked for today. Nevertheless, we need it urgently in order to cope with our lives and to confront the problems of our world with hope. Therefore I wish you the Angel of Patience, so that you do not give up at once if you are in a difficult situation and the problem seems insoluble. May the Angel of Patience give you the power to carry something through and the confidence that change will happen.

THE ANGEL OF LIGHTNESS

POPE JOHN XXIII once wrote in his journal, "Giovanni, don't take yourself so seriously!" He handled himself with a grace that the Angel of Lightness can teach you. Sure, we need to tackle big problems. For this we need the Angel of Courage. But especially with personal problems, confronting them head on is not always the answer. The more fiercely we attack our shortcomings, the more resistance we tend to meet. And we end up in endless battle. Then Pope John XXIII's light touch might appease us. He was a pope much more relaxed than many before him who might have appeared likely to collapse under the weight of this office. But it was Pope John XXIII who had the courage to call a Council –a consultative meeting of all the bishops and many of the leading theologians from around the world that took place in Rome in the 1960s and set the Catholic Church's course for the future.

Yes, especially when dealing with ourselves we need a touch of Lightness. Often we get stuck within ourselves because we take ourselves so seriously. We cannot forgive ourselves for faulty traits we think we should have overcome by now. So we make a concerted effort to eradicate these mistakes. But the more fiercely we strike, the stronger they seem to grow. In the end we lack the necessary patience, and we either treat ourselves even more harshly or we give up the struggle. The Angel of Lightness suggests another way: not to condone our faulty behavior, but to combat it with humor. We need not make a catastrophe out of failing and failing again. We can take our human weaknesses lightly; we do not have to take it all upon ourselves, because we know that we are in God's hands. When we think that we have to resolve everything, responsibility weighs us down and we experience our human being as heavy. Lightness does not mean light-headedness or carelessness. Rather it is based on our profound faith that we are in God's good hands and that He takes care of us. We know that we do not have to prove anything to God. Then it is not so terrible if we fail, because God won't be disappointed by our failure. When we do not meet our own expectations, we upset only ourselves.

The Angel of Lightness also calls us into a new freedom when relating to others. Anyone who, like me, lives in a monastic community knows that we do better when not meeting everything with dead seriousness; otherwise we artificially complicate our daily lives. We continued to be flawed human beings when entering a monastery and, indeed, that is true for everybody else as well. Every mother knows not to constantly upset herself about her children's shortcomings. She, too, needs the lightness that grows from her trust that eventually the children will get over their childishness and grow up. After all, they are children. They are supposed to make mistakes so that they can learn from them.

Children who experience this lightness in their parents will develop a stronger confidence in life than can children whose parents take everything with gravity, as if parenting was like getting a Ph.D., or taking a test one must pass. If we attempt to raise the perfect children, we might end up achieving quite the opposite.

This lightness of a parent also comes from the confidence that children are not just our own children, and they don't only depend on my "perfect" parenting. Our children also belong in God's hands. God sends his angel to care for every child.

If we look at the angels rejoicing over the nativity scene, or the putti of baroque paintings, we can feel something of the lightness they radiate. They do not take life as seriously as we do. They know to fly and hover over many things that we cling to, those things that we are determined to sort out at all costs. Often artists have depicted these angels as youthful and childlike, playful, inwardly free and content — they understood

this lightness of the angels. Among these angels resides also the angel of lightness who
is calling us to lose the weightiness of life
and to give us a lightness of being.

THE ANGEL OF OPENNESS

OFTEN WE CANNOT TRULY ENCOUNTER another person because we are locked inside ourselves. We build defenses around ourselves, so that no one can get through. We hide out behind masks we have constructed, so no one can discover our true face. We don't want to reveal ourselves because we fear true encounters. We dread our own truth. The Angel of Openness calls us to open ourselves to the mystery of truly meeting another person. We can only meet other people when we are open to them, when we open our hearts and allow them in. For me, the archetype of such openness is the meeting between Mary and Elizabeth as told in the gospel of Luke (Luke 1). There we read that Mary sets out; she leaves her home, the place where she is protected, and crosses a mountain range. She traverses the mountains of prejudice, which often prevent us from meeting others; she passes over the peaks of inhibitions, which keep us from going out of ourselves. She then goes into the house of her cousin Elizabeth and greets her. She doesn't offer this greeting from outside the house, but she enters her home, which symbolized her heart. They both are open to each other. Thus they experience the mystery of true encounter and both are transformed, that is, both touch upon the original image in which God has made them. There the child in Elizabeth's womb leaps up in joy, for he reminds her of the un-

adulaterated image of God within her. And
she recognizes the mother of her Master.
And in a song of praise, the so-called Mag
nificat, Mary expresses the mystery of her
life. She understands that God has looked
upon the lowliness of His servant and done

great things through her. When we encounter another person as openly as symbolized in the story of Mary and Elizabeth, we will be transformed and shown the mystery of our life.

May the Angel of Openness open you up for the future, for what God has in store for you. Often we settle ourselves so firmly into our lives that we are no longer open to anything new that God may bring. We want everything to stay the same. We become like fossils. But you want to be open to the new possibilities God wants to give you. New things can only flourish in your life when you become open to them, when you stop clinging to the old, when you do not freeze in your life as it currently is. This openness shows itself in a readiness to take on new ideas, to learn new ways of behaving, to meet new challenges at work, in your family, and in society. Open people are prepared to keep learning new things in their profession and embrace new technology and developments. Open people remain awake and alive.

Openness in relating to others also means uprightness and honesty. When you speak your opinion openly to others, they know where you stand. When we are open in this way, we become a blessing to others. Then we will not speak about others behind their backs. But others can open up in our presence. Our uprightness does others good as well. Even if we have to say unpleasant things, others can understand that we mean well. Then we do not hide our preconceptions and prejudices behind a facade. We show ourselves as we are. We dare to tell the truth because we feel free. Then we are not dependent on others agreeing. When others cannot bear our constructive critique, if we are at peace with ourselves, we can take it. May the Angel of Openness give you such uprightness and honesty that you can share your truth with complete inner freedom. Of course, such uprightness requires savvy and sensitivity. You must sense where you can say something without unnecessarily hurting the other person. Yet when you are not depending on being popular at all costs, you become free to tell the truth. Look at the way the Angel Gabriel tells Mary about the birth of her Son. Artists have consistently painted this Angel as very open and forthcoming. Gabriel reveals to Mary something completely new and implausible. With his openness he opens Mary to the apparently impossible. May the Angel of Openness open you up to the mystery of encountering another human person and to new things you are completely capable of.

THE ANGEL OF SOBRIETY

WE MAY USE THE WORD 'SOBER' to mean dull and dreary. But this is definitely not where the Angel of Sobriety would lead you. In the monastery we have three nightly prayer services or night watches. These take place before breakfast, and we have not yet eaten anything. When you have not yet eaten, you are sober and wide awake; you are aware of things as they really are. When we drink a lot, our mind becomes foggy and we have only a faint grasp of reality. When we eat a lot, we are filled up, groggy, and incapable of taking in very much. Sobriety then means seeing things as they are, without looking at them through sleepy eyes or projections.

Sobriety is needed when in a heated discussion people are taken over by their emotions. Sobriety is a blessing, when a decision must be taken and a clear sight of things is blocked out by power struggles or destructive relationship dynamics. A craftsman once told me about working in a convent. One of the nuns wanted a yellow curtain, not because she liked it but because Mother Superior wanted it, and because another nun, whom she disliked, had wished for a green curtain. Quite often our decisions are affected by such relational issues. At such time the Angel of Sobriety calls us to look with clarity for the right solution. Sobriety also means objectivity and truth to the facts. When we are true to the facts of reality, we are also true to the One who is the foundation of that very reality.

But often we mix up the facts with our emotions, and we no longer see well. Then we flounder in a morass of emotions, cannot get out on our own, and become incapable of tackling any issue or conflict.

The Angel of Sobriety will be a blessing to you when someone is seeking your advice, when others share with you their problems, wounds, and disappointments. If you can avoid getting pulled into the quagmire of emotions but somberly shed light on what this specific situation is all about, then you can truly help. Then you can help the other person to find their way out of the emotional entanglement. Sobriety requires a certain distance from the other person. When you are awash with sympathy, you become unable to show the way. At first your compassion can be beneficial to the other person, but it is not enough just to have a good grumble together about how awful life is. You need to develop empathy, yet you also need to take a sober look from a fair distance, in order to find a way out of the jungle of problems.

The Angel of Sobriety can also help you to assess your own situation better. Then you can let go of exaggerations and drama and find ways to sort things out. Sometimes you have blinders on and see things only in terms of your own anger, disappointment, or hurt. But that prevents you from finding sensible solutions. I wish you the Angel of Sobriety, so that you can clear up your own situation, and you may bring clarity into the fog of conflict that confuses human relationships and decisions.

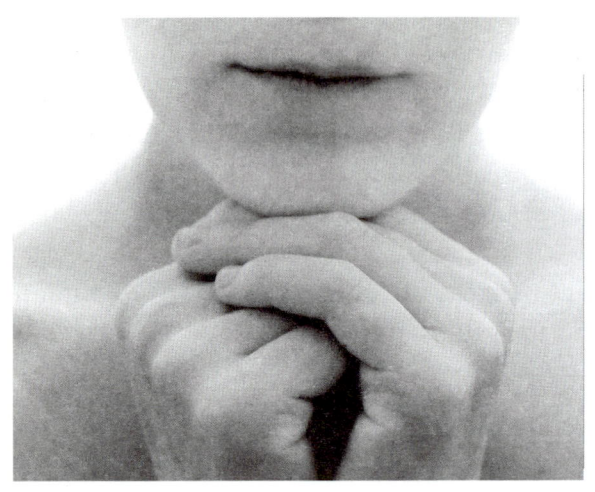

THE ANGEL
OF FORGIVENESS

W E MAY ASSOCIATE FORGIVENESS and pardon with being soft and submissive. Others may then take advantage of us. Particularly for Christians, there seems to be nothing we can do except to forgive. We are not supposed to defend ourselves but are called to forgive even our worst enemy. The Angel of Forgiveness does not want you to be humiliated or leave you defenseless. The Angel of Forgiveness wants to free you from the power of people who have injured and hurt you.

You are not being asked to suppress your own feelings when you forgive someone. Forgiveness happens when anger ends, not when it begins. In order to forgive, first you need to feel the hurt the other person has caused you. Do not wallow in it, or you will hurt yourself more. For this you need to allow yourself anger just as you need to become aware of the pain. Let your anger toward the person who hurt you rise up from within. Anger is the energy that puts distance between you and the one who hurt you. Anger enables you to cast out from within you the person who hurt and upset you. Only once out of your emotional space will you be able to reflect: "This person is just a human being, a child that has been hurt just like me." Or you can pray like Jesus on the cross: "Father, forgive them, for they know not what they do" (Luke 23:34).

Perhaps others think that they know what they are doing when they hurt us — when they want to make us feel guilty or criticize us mercilessly, exposing our most sensitive spots. And in a sense they do know what they are doing. Yet, most likely they do not understand the full measure of pain they are causing us. Someone might be so enmeshed in their own ways, fear, and despair that they must make you small, so they can believe in their own greatness. Feeling inferior might cause them to put down another so that they themselves can feel bigger.

Once you understand this, the other person has no more power over you. Only when through your anger you free yourself from another person's power can you really forgive. Then you feel that forgiveness does you good, that ultimately it is forgiveness that liberates you from the power of those who hurt you.

It can take a long while before we can really forgive. But we ought not disregard our feelings. For example, if your father keeps hurting you, first you need anger in order to distance yourself from him. Possibly this anger first must grow stronger so that his putting you down, his constant criticism can no longer reach you. As long as the knife that pierced you is wedged into your flesh, you cannot forgive. You would only injure yourself more with it. You would push it further into the wound. That would be masochism. Only when you cast out the other person from within you can you truly forgive. Otherwise forgiveness would merely mean to give up on yourself, to resign yourself to dire fate. But at some point we need to forgive. We will never get away from those who hurt us if we do not forgive. Forgiveness frees us from the hurts others have caused us. And forgiveness heals our wounds.

Once at a workshop I invited participants to think of three people who had caused them pain. I asked everybody to allow themselves to feel the pain and the anger, and then to forgive these three people. At the moment I heard the stories, I understood the extent to which we walk through life bearing our deep old wounds. We need the Angel of Forgiveness, so that our wounds heal and we become free of people who otherwise would still have power over us. Unforgiven injuries cripple us. They use up energy that we need to live. We may not get healthy because of the wounds that remain unforgiven. But the Angel of Forgiveness allows us time. We are not asked to do more than we can do.

As human beings we cannot exist together without forgiveness, because whether we want to or not, we keep hurting one another. If we keep counting our injuries, we enter a vicious circle. If we ignore them, they generate bitterness and aggression in us; and at whatever inopportune moment we can explode with violent reproaches, criticism, and resentment. At some time, we will get back at the other. And one trespass engenders another. The Angel of Forgiveness breaks the vicious circle of reproach. The Angel of Forgiveness clears the air and empowers us — us who are hurt and who hurt others time and again — to live together in peace.

THE ANGEL OF FREEDOM

W E ALL LONG FOR FREEDOM. We hurt when we feel dependent. When other people control us, when in their presence we feel obligated, we become angry. It offends our dignity. The same is true when our emotions or our habits control us — we then feel uncomfortable. In most places today we do have an outer political freedom. Yet in our personal relationships we often don't feel free. We may feel limited by certain constraints. We feel governed by societal expectations. We don't dare to break out and swim against the current. We feel determined by others. We may not feel free to say what we think. We wonder what others will think about us, and act according to what we imagine they'll like. But this way I cannot become my own person; I will never discover who I really am.

The English word 'freedom' comes from the Indo-European root *prai*, which means to protect, to look after, to care for, and to love. The early Germanic peoples called anyone they loved and therefore protected a free person. This person was entitled to dwell freely and with equal rights in the community — free, unrestricted, and independent. I feel free when I feel loved. Then I do not need to adapt myself to another person's expectations. I can be who I am. When I feel loved by someone, in his or her presence I can be as I feel. I need not fear what the other person thinks of me. I know that

I am accepted. When I know I am loved in the depths of my being, I am free from the pressure to fill other people's expectations. I am free from always having to be success-ful, always having to prove something, and having to meet society's standards.

Interestingly, the ancient Greeks had three words for freedom. *Eleutheria* means the freedom to go where I like, to be free to act, to do what I feel is right for me, not to be constrained by the rules and expectations of others. *Parrhesia* means freedom of speech. Today we may not see this as anything special. In a democracy we can say what we think. And yet we are not always free. I know, for example, of an extraordinarily gifted person with excellent references who nevertheless has a hard time finding a job. At every interview his whole focus goes into worrying about what the HR director might think of his words. Will they consider him to be neurotic if he were to use this word or that? Even though he is free to say whatever he wants, he is not free in his speech. We are only free when we can show ourselves as we are, when we can express our truth to others. The third Greek word, *autarkia*, means self-rule or self-determination. I can decide for myself what I want, what I eat and how much, and when I refrain or fast. This inner feeling of freedom, of being my own master, is an essential part of human dignity. Today we are often driven by our cravings. Here the Angel of Freedom can lift us up and help us freely to determine ourselves.

There is the story of a woman who has fallen in love with a man. But he is not interested. Although she knows that the relationship has no chance and will end up hurting her, she cannot break away. The Angel of Freedom calls upon her to restore her dignity, so that she may feel valued from within and does not need to run after this man. We may also feel constrained and unfree in our marriage, family, or community. We have no space to breathe. Then the Angel of Freedom wants to give us an inner freedom that allows us to feel free even under constrained circumstances. This inner freedom tells us that no one has power over our true self. It gives us independence even in friendship. Then I don't define myself in other people's terms; I am always myself. Such freedom is essential for friendship or marriage to succeed. When two people cling to one another, and constantly need to check what the other person is thinking, a mature relationship cannot develop.

In every commitment to another person, you still need your own freedom. When you bind yourself you do so in freedom. You leave yourself a space that no one else can dispose of. My wish for you is that the Angel of Freedom may give you this inner freedom so that you can experience yourself as free and live as an upright person.

THE ANGEL OF PARTING

PARTING IS PAINFUL. Saying goodbye to someone you love can break your heart. But parting must be. We cannot hold on to each other. We need to go our own way for our lives to succeed. Life brings a thousand goodbyes. We have to part from familiar surroundings, because we may want to study in a faraway city or because we have found work somewhere else. Every change requires parting. But our goodbyes need to be successful if we want to really involve ourselves in the next thing; only then can something new grow in us. Yet we'd like to hold on to everybody we've become close to. We want to keep every friendship going forever. But some friendships last just a while. Then they become a drag. We may prolong them out of a sense of duty or so as not to hurt the other person. But things aren't right. It is time to say goodbye. Doing so I am also being fair to the other person. I trust that this friend can find a new direction as well. And then I am free to begin anew.

There is one kind of parting that is particularly painful. It is parting from a husband, wife, or partner with whom we had planned to spend our life. Today many of us suffer this painful parting. Relationships break up. A marriage cannot go on because two people are only hurting each other, making life together hell. There are situations when we need to truly part or we end up fighting out our departures in court, endlessly remaining at war. Love turns to hate. Here a parting ritual developed by therapists can help us to say goodbye properly. We certainly want to put into words all the good experiences we have had with the other person; we want to express our gratitude for everything he or she has given us. Only then can we say why, despite all this, we must part. So we can both go our own way, without having to write off the years of life we spent together. We can gratefully accept our times together and then go forward in freedom, without bitterness, reproaches, or self-laceration.

But we don't have to say goodbye only to people. We have to say goodbye to habits, life phases, and life patterns. If you have never said goodbye to your childhood, you will always keep nurturing infantile wishes. If you have never said goodbye to puberty, you will always be prey to the illusions we then had about life. We have to say goodbye to our youth if we want to grow up, to our bachelorhood if we want to get married, to our job when we retire. But above all we must say goodbye to the injuries we have suffered during the course of our life. We cannot live a good life when we hang on to the hurt we suffered in childhood. Otherwise as adults we may still blame our parents for their limitations in our upbringing, and for not meeting all of our needs. If you want to live in the here and now and fully conscious, you must say goodbye to the injuries you suffered in childhood. Here and now you are responsible for your life. It does not matter what your childhood was like; now you can make something of what was given you. We never have only good or only bad experiences. Even with all the wounds, our parents have also given us healthy roots. But we can only discover them when we intentionally part from our parents.

May the Angel of Parting help you to say goodbye to old life patterns that make your life difficult — for example, the pattern of perfectionism, which compels us to control everything, or the pattern of self-criticism, which drives us always to blame ourselves and put ourselves down. We must let go of the pattern of perfect performance solely to prove our worth to our mother. Possibly your mother's place has been taken over by a school or church authority, and you wear yourself out for them. But it is still the same old pattern. If we do not part from old life patterns, they drive us to hurt either ourselves or others, or to subconsciously seek out situations that continue our childhood hurts. You may then find yourself with a boss who puts you down in exactly the same way your father did. Or you find a girlfriend who is as possessive as your mother was. May the Angel of Parting help you to say goodbye to your past and useless life patterns, so that you may fully live in the present, realize your potential, and allow you to develop in new and amazing ways.

THE ANGEL OF MOURNING

THE WORD 'MOURNING' immediately evokes the thought of mourning for a loved one who has died. This is the most solemn mourning. When we do not mourn a loved one who passed, a mother or father, for example, we block the flow of our life. We may not understand why we cannot really enjoy life, what it is that prevents us from living fully. This may come from not having mourned. In mourning we intentionally focus on the loss of this person's life. We recall our relationship with him or her. We remember the experiences we shared, what the person meant to us, what he or she gave us. Yet we do not disregard the difficulties we may have experienced, the pain we may have suffered, and those things we may have never expressed or affirmed. We may be taken aback when anger shows up in our mourning. But this is okay. Mourning clarifies our relationship and sets it on a new level. Once we have gone through mourning, we can build a new relationship with a deceased loved ones, and they can become inner companions. They have not simply disappeared. We may encounter them in a special dream. They may communicate helpful words. Or they remind us that we are in need of a certain quality their life represented. In mourning we discover who the other person really was. During their life on this earth we knew them only in part. Another part was hidden behind their mask. Only after death do we understand how they wanted to live, what was the deepest longing of their heart, what was the mission they wanted to bring.

But the Angel of Mourning not only calls you to mourn properly for the dead. Often this angel wants to teach you the art of purifying and letting go the past.

There is mourning for all the life you have not lived. At some point in our lives we may feel that life tricked us. We were never able to live the life we wanted. Our parents and teachers may have pushed us in a direction that wasn't right for us. Or we come to understand what our childhood was really like — maybe we never felt safe in our family. To acknowledge this is very painful and needs mourning. Otherwise these disappointments may control us or creep into all of our thinking and doing. We may not realize why we react with such hypersensitivity in certain situations or simply freeze up. It is our life's disappointments that we have not rightfully mourned.

However, we do not suffer disappointments only in childhood. Throughout life we experience relationships breaking up and our lives being smashed. We fail. All the ideals we wanted to fulfill have proved to be illusions. We find ourselves disillusioned and without energy. A man once told me that after the breakup of a relationship he felt as if his wings had been cut off. The Angel of Mourning wants to protect you from going through life with clipped wings. You are called to receive new wings, so that you can fly into the air and look at your disappointments from above. The Angel of Mourning gives you new energy to take on the tasks that are now before you. However, the Angel of Mourning cannot protect you from the pain that comes with every mourning. You must face this pain. But you can rest assured that you are not alone; the Angel of Mourning accompanies you and transforms your pain into new life. The Angel of Mourning may also send you people who can be with you in your sadness — friends who understand you, who can feel with you and open your eyes to new possibilities that now are before you.

THE ANGEL
OF TRANSFORMATION

ANGELS COME ALONG IN DIFFERENT clothing. They possess the art of transformation. They can change into a human being to accompany us on our way. They become a doctor who heals our wounds, a therapist who pulls us out of neurotic patterns, a minister who releases us from our self-judgment. "Angels come out of the blue," says a modern song. Your friend may say something that makes you see everything in a new light. A child may look at you and show you just how little relevance the problems have that are racking your brain.

Angels are quick-change artists. But the Angel of Transformation calls you into the mystery of your own transformation. If you want to stay alive, you have to keep changing. What doesn't change dies. The psychologist Carl Jung once said that the greatest enemy of change is a successful life, because when we are successful we tend to find everything in order. We see no need for change. But then we stand still, both outwardly and inwardly. We speak the same way we have for the last twenty years. We resort to the same solutions, which have always worked for us. But we become boring. There is little pleasure in being with us. Our speaking and our thinking grows stale, like cold coffee that has lost its aroma.

But the Angel of Transformation also wants to keep you from being too hard on yourself. Our wish to fix ourselves can carry a lot of harshness and self-rejection. We think we must become a different person. We think we are no good the way we are. We want finally to overcome our faults, super-sensitivity, fear, or bad temper. But inherent in such resolution is the idea that all my faults and weaknesses are bad. The Angel of Transformation is calling you to the truth that everything in you is good, that everything in you has a right to exist and is meaningful. Yet it also needs to be transformed. Your fear is good. It can show you that your life is based on false premises. You may want to be perfect in everything and avoid mistakes at all cost. Your fear can show you how hurtful this attitude is. Fear can invite you to adopt a more generous approach to life. Your anger is good. If you listen to it, if you get to the bottom of it, your anger can become transformed into new life energy. Your anger may show you that you have always geared yourself toward others. Now you finally want to live your own life. Then your anger transforms into life energy.

The old fairy tales knew about the mystery of transformation. In these stories human beings become animals and animals change into human beings. Everything can transform into something else. This tells us we need not be afraid of anything that we may find inside ourselves. Within you, too, everything can be transformed. There is one beautiful fairy tale in particular that describes the mystery of transformation. It is the tale of the three languages. In it a young man does not learn what his father wants him to learn. But he learns the language of barking dogs, the language of frogs, and the language of birds. When in his wanderings he comes to a castle, the lord of the castle offers him only the tower in which wild barking dogs, who have already gobbled up many others, are kenneled. The young man is not afraid because

he understands the language of dogs. These dogs tell him that the reason for their fierce behavior is a treasure they guard. They show him the treasure and help him to dig it up. Then they disappear, and peace comes to the land. I like this story. Precisely where your main problem lies, where you make yourself suffer the most, where you are sick, there also lies your treasure. There you may touch your true self. The story tells us that everything within us has a meaning. When we are constantly discontented and angry, this does not mean you should reject yourself. But you should then ask yourself what treasure these feelings are pointing you toward. Once you dig up your treasure, once you have found your true self, those emotions will transform, and you will be

at peace. You'll be grateful that the barking dog pushed your attention to the hidden
treasure. May the Angel of Transformation
give you the courage to treat yourself gently,
because everything in you is material for
transformation, until finally your true self
shines through.

THE ANGEL OF INSPIRATION

I FIND INSPIRED PEOPLE REFRESHING. When we are inspired we may have a clever thought, let's say about rearranging our work, and we get excited about that. Or we travel on a vacation and admire a new landscape with great enthusiasm. We can get inspired by an evening out with friends. New ideas inspire us, and we sweep others along with our enthusiasm. When we let ourselves be inspired, we experience everything with intensity. We point out to each other how wonderfully the sun is shining through the clouds, how extraordinarily beautiful a mountain is, towering over the valley.

On the other hand we can get to a point when we no longer feel inspired about anything. Then on a vacation we might travel further and further away, yet when asked about that trip we immediately start complaining about how we didn't like the food or disapproved of the service in the hotel. Without inspiration we constantly need new effects from the outside just to feel like ourselves. But the further we travel and the more money we spend, the less we really experience, the less alive we feel. We seek life outside of ourselves because inside we have no life. Yet what we do encounter we don't let in, and so we become unable to experience anything intensely. We are inspired when we can be moved by a word, a look, a meeting, or the park we walk, or the mountain we climb. We feel inspired by looking at a beautiful landscape. Then we let ourselves be drawn out of our aloofness. We get out of ourselves and into whatever we are experiencing. The ancient Greeks used the word 'ecstasy' to mean getting out of ourselves, and they used the word 'inspiration' to mean being in God. So ultimately inspiration means letting myself be drawn into the One whom I encounter in everything — in creation, in every human being, in every word, in music, and in art. Only in God can I experience the whole mystery of a human being, nature, and art. In God I experience the full depth of being. In everything I ultimately come to touch God.

When we are inspired we inspire others. We radiate life. We don't just sit around in the evening moaning about things. We sparkle with enthusiasm. We have good ideas and want to take others along. We share our experiences with enthusiasm, and things become lively and fresh. We don't just exchange meaningless chatter but have real conversations. New ideas come up, new plans are drawn up. A new pleasure in life awakens within us. And suddenly we find the energy to go to a concert, visit a museum, take a hike. Then we may enliven and inspire others.

My wish for you is that the Angel of Inspiration will inspire you to be moved by who you meet, by what you experience, and by who you are. I wish that you may also motivate others to follow you in an idea or a project, that you may enliven and inspire them. Then the Angel of Inspiration will give you a new joy in life and transform you to be yourself an Angel of Inspiration to the people you meet.

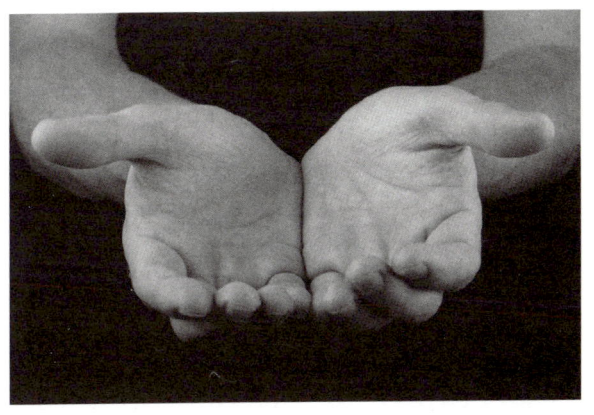

THE ANGEL OF HEALING

W E ASSOCIATE THE WORD 'HEALING' primarily with the idea of health and the curing of sickness. The word 'to heal' is rooted in an old Germanic word meaning well, hale, saved, whole, complete, fresh, or unweakened. As a noun it meant happiness, health, healing, help, or salvation. The Angel of Healing calls you to hope that your life will succeed, that it may become whole, that you can accept everything that is in you, say yes to everything you are, and honestly feel that "it is good as it is."

For you to say this, you must first heal your wounds. Each of us bears wounds. We might have been hurt by our parents, even when they meant more than well. We might have gotten hurt if we were not taken seriously as a unique person, if our desires and feelings were simply ignored, or if our fundamental need for love, safety, and reliability was not fulfilled. We may have been hurt by teachers when they made us look foolish in front of the class, or by priests and pastors who attempted to fill us with the fear of hell. We might get hurt by a boyfriend or girlfriend when we quarrel, when we touch each other's sensitivities, or when we put a knife into the other's old wounds. The Angel of Healing tells you: Wounds can heal and will heal. Of course, healing a wound does not mean you simply do not feel them anymore. But they won't go on to fester.

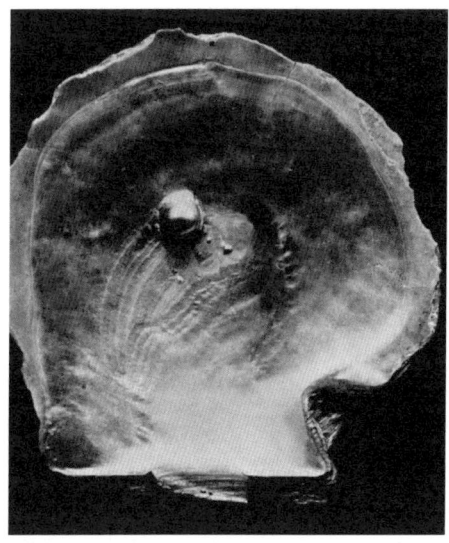

Scars will grow around them. Then they become a part of you, without holding you back in your life. They will no longer use up all your energy. Indeed, your wounds will keep you perceptive and become a source of life for you. With the Angel of Healing your wounds can become a precious treasure, a prized pearl, as the medieval nun and doctor Hildegard of Bingen said. Where you were wounded, there you will be open for the people around you; you will respond caringly when others tell you about their own wounds. There you will be alive. There you get in touch with yourself, with your true self.

May the Angel of Healing give you the hope that all your wounds can heal. May the Angel of Healing restore you so that you may not merely be defined by the history of your injuries, but that fully you may live in the present, because now your wounds no longer prevent you from living. They may even help you to live. The Angel of Healing offers to transform your wounds into a source of life and a blessing for yourself and others.

Once the Angel of Healing has healed your wounds, you yourself will become an Angel of Healing for others. Then others will feel good when they are with you. They will sense that it is okay to show you their wounds, because you will understand — you will not judge but simply accept. This way you create a healing environment. You do not project your wounds onto others. You don't talk others into your own problems and you can really listen. Then others can share their grievances without fear that you may brand them as sick or as mere moaners. You may not even realize why people like to come to you and why they speak to you so openly. The Angel of Healing who transformed your wounds now wishes to share with others, in you and through you, the good news: You are good just as you are. You are whole and healthy and all your wounds can heal.

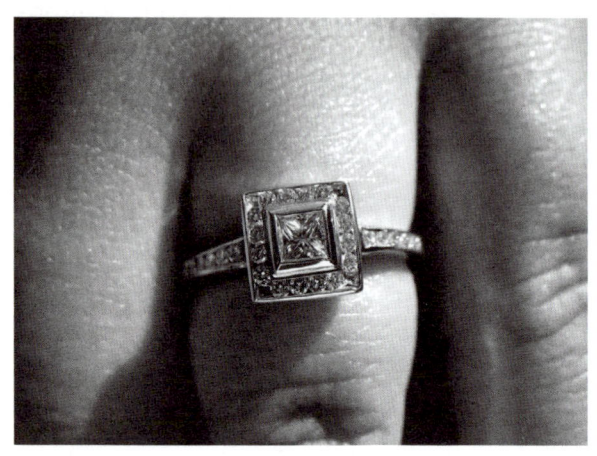

THE ANGEL
OF FAITHFULNESS

FAITHFULNESS ISN'T IN HIGH DEMAND these days. Too often we have witnessed a bride and a groom pledge to be eternally faithful, only to see their marriage break down before long. We are afraid to promise our faithfulness to another person, because we know well that there is no guarantee for our emotions. Yet we long for people who are faithful, who stand by us and give us protection and assurance. Our longing for others to be faithful to us corresponds to our doubts about our own ability to be faithful.

The English word 'true' corresponds to the Germanic word *treu* which today means faithful, but originally meant steadfast or strong as a tree. But often we do not feel as steadfast as a tree, which has deep roots and cannot be easily toppled. We fear that we cannot be faithful to each other, that we cannot give any guarantee about ourselves. Faithfulness does not simply mean being true to one's principles or objectives. That is simply fulfilling one's duty. Faithfulness eventually means being faithful to *You*, being faithful to a person. Faithfulness requires love. We can only be faithful to someone we love. Faithfulness contains our longing to entrust everything to the person we love, to stay open to the call of the person we have committed to. Faithfulness isn't something static, but it is my readiness to walk with another person, and my promise to be faithful and reliable even as I keep changing. It is in faithfulness, as I commit to the future, that I bathe myself in the light of life's possibilities.

The philosopher Otto Bollnow tells us that as human persons we come into our own only through faithfulness, where in life's constant ebb and flow we find the steady core of our own personhood. When we promise to be faithful to another person we cannot guarantee that promise. Neither should we. With my monastic vows I promised faithfulness to our community of monks.

I have no guarantee that one day I may fall so madly in love that I can no longer live in this community. But I am helped by God's assurance that He is faithful. The Second Letter to Timothy in the New Testament offers these words that I find most comforting: "When we are faithless, He remains faithful, for He cannot renounce himself" (2:13). God remains faithful to me, even if I am not faithful. This gives me the certainty that my life will succeed, even if it fractures inwardly and outwardly. And this takes away my fear of fully committing myself to my community.

When we say someone is faithful, we do not just talk about spouses who are faithful in their marriage and do not stray. We also mean people we can rely on. We need not keep courting their favor. They stand with us faithfully, and that does us good. We know we can count on them even if we may not hear from them for a while. We may write to a friend just once a year, yet stay in touch for decades. Not because we feel obligated but because this friend is important to us, and we look for ways to keep in touch and meet up when possible. For example, my sister once travelled to Italy as a young woman. There she met a professor of sociology, a married man. They each went their own way, yet through all the ups and downs of life they have kept in touch for over 30 years. Still today, whenever my sister travels to Italy she is welcome there, and if her friend happens to be away himself she gets the key to his apartment. They have developed a kind of faithfulness that is reliable and does them good.

Faithfulness need not be put forward in flashy oaths of loyalty. It expresses itself in your being reliable, and in your readiness to stand by others throughout their lives, walking with them through all the changes life brings, never turning the other way. Blessings lie upon such faithfulness. We comprehend the angel who empowers us to be that faithful. For by ourselves we cannot be so. It is such faithfulness that carries and sustains us in this unsteady world. Then we know that we are important to someone. That helps us to see our own value and to stand by ourselves in spite of all our disappointments. My wish for you is that the Angel of Faithfulness may be at your side and that people come to you upon whom you can rely. May the Angel of Faithfulness also empower you to be faithful. Then you will be good for others, and you will find your true self amid the irritable fancies of your heart.

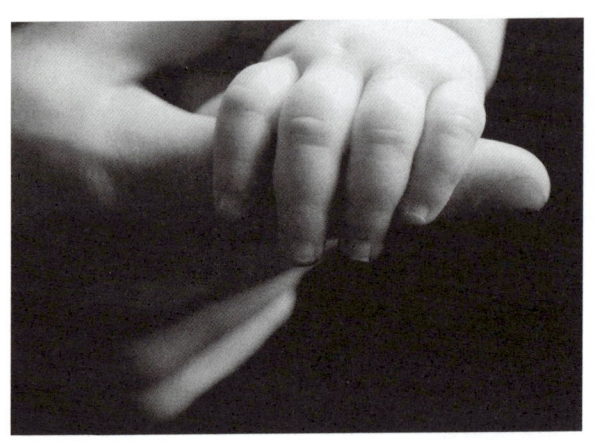

THE ANGEL
OF TENDERNESS

WHEN I LOVE, I could experience the other person to be to me an angel of great tenderness. Thus we express how good we feel when another embraces us not as property but like a beloved treasure which requires gentle care. But tenderness is not only the way two people treat each other when they are in love. Tenderness has become a modern virtue. In the midst of a world dominated by violence, we yearn for a different way of relating to each other. We long for an air of tenderness. We strive to create our own culture of tenderness, our own lifestyle of tenderness. Tenderness is the art of treating with tender care another person, nature, and all things. While the idea of tenderness is a specifically modern concept, we find the phenomenon of tenderness throughout all ages. The Bible is full of tender encounters. The Letter to Titus in the New Testament tells us that God's tenderness has been revealed in Jesus Christ (Tit. 3:4). The writer Heinrich Boll, author of the Irish Journal, called for a theology of tenderness, and he found in the Bible a theology of tenderness, a tenderness "that always heals."

The Angel of Tenderness calls us to practice the art of treating people delicately and tenderly, and not only people but everything we deal with. The word 'tender' can mean loving, beloved, valuable, close, delicate, beautiful, and soft. We can treat others tenderly only when we have come to love them. Then we will not force them, criticize them, or treat them with aggression. Then we will not pressure them to share their secrets. Then we will treat them with care. We will speak tenderly and act gently. When others feel thus respected and precious, so that they may discover their own beauty, tenderness dares to express itself in tender gestures, a gentle touch, a tender caressing, a fleeing kiss. Then love flows between us, a love that does not hold tight and makes no claim to possess, but one that knows to set free, a love that shows respect and is attentive to the other person's mystery.

There is a way to handle all things tenderly. So when I pick up a book, I hold it carefully in my hands, because it is precious to me. It takes me aback to see books

being handled brutally. They might get read and thrown aside. Psychologists claim that brutality is often an expression of repressed sexuality. Tenderness is the expression of an integrated sexuality. Then our sexuality flows into everything we do in life, everything we touch, all the work we do, all our dealings with people and things. Then we treat the cup and saucer tenderly when we put them on the table. Tenderly we pick up the tool we are going to work with. The great monk and founder of Western monasticism, Saint Benedict of Nursia, required the administrator of the monastery to treat all tools like altar vessels. Ultimately in everything we touch we touch the Creator.

I wish that you may meet Angels of Tenderness, who treat you tenderly, and who give you an atmosphere of tenderness where you can flourish, be wholly yourself, let go of yourself, and simply feel fine. And I wish for you that you may become an Angel of Tenderness for others. For this you must first go to school with the Angel of Tenderness. Then go and be tender with all you meet, and everything you touch. A tender space you will create around yourself, one where others feel protected.

THE ANGEL OF CHEER

OR THE EARLY MONKS, CHEERFULNESS and inner clarity, merriment and brightness were the signs of a harmonious spirituality. When we know our own truth when we have experienced our ups and downs, and once we feel completely accepted, cheer shines forth. We no longer walk through the world with a gloomy face. Nothing human is foreign to us. We know that everything is in safe hands — our own weakness and the flawed ways of humanity. There is a glow radiating from within us as we are illuminated completely by the healing, warming light of divine love. Cheerful people radiate a bright light upon their surroundings. It drives away the clouds that darken human minds.

Cheerfulness is not just a disposition we are born with. It arises from deep trust that we are unconditionally accepted as we are, that ultimately all is good. And it arises from the courage to behold our own truth. Christians are convinced that only when we let the light of God penetrate into the abyss of our souls will we shine with cheer. There are no dark places in us that we must hide, no void to terrify us. We walk worry-free. This is not naive optimism but an attitude that springs from encountering the truth. Once we've looked our own truth in the eye, we need no longer agonize over potential troubles and dangers. We don't obsess over the dark side of this world, but we see everything bathed in divine light. Then we can be confident that this light, which has won in our hearts, will also prevail in the world.

Such cheer is infectious. In the presence of a cheerful person one will not talk about the end of the world. One won't indulge in bemoaning the terrors of this earth. As cheerful people we do not shut our eyes to reality. We don't repress the dark side of things. But we see things from a different perspective. This ultimately is the perspective of the spirit who looks all through the darkness to eventually find the bright light of God. We see everything from the perspective of angels — angels who see this world's reality as it is, yet rise above it on wings and, despite all difficulty, regard it with an inner cheer.

A cheerful person cannot be scared easily. When we are

cheerful we are at peace with ourselves. Nothing can upset us easily. When you talk to a cheerful person you begin to feel cheerful yourself. You see yourself and your life with new eyes. It feels good to be with cheerful people. And we all know how depressing it can be to be with someone who looks at everything with gloom, who is obsessed with the negative, and sees it everywhere. Cheerful people brighten us. Suddenly we feel lighter. I wish that you may meet many Angels of Cheer. Likewise, I wish that the Angel of Cheerfulness will make you feel bright inside so that you become cheerful and light, shining and cloudless, and the world around you also becomes brilliant and cheerful.

THE ANGEL OF DEDICATION

CHILDREN DEVOTE THEMSELVES to play with total dedication. Nothing can disturb them. In their play they forget themselves. They give themselves up to the game. The old artists of the baroque period of European culture often represented angels as children who are playing with perfect dedication. The Christmas angel painted by Matthias Grünewald on the famous Isenheim altar is completely lost in the violin playing. The art historian Wilhelm Fraenger says that for Grünewald angels are "vessels of heavenly joy and rapture ... the quintessence of overflowing bliss." In art, angels are masters of dedication. They are completely in the moment — they devote themselves wholly to whatever they do. The story is told of a Jewish Rabbi. It was said that the most important thing for him was whatever he was doing at the moment. Clearly he had been initiated by the Angel of Dedication to give himself so fully to the moment.

Researchers dedicate themselves to their work. They do not let go until the solution is found. Craftspeople carry out their work with dedication. But ultimately, dedication pertains especially to two areas of life: dedication to love, in sexuality, and mystical dedication to God. Dedication in love can show most clearly what dedication means. The sexual act is designed to be the climax of complete dedication. Both lovers forget about themselves and dedicate completely to the other person, give themselves to the other, melting into one. When we dedicate ourselves fully to another person we give up holding onto ourselves. We no longer cling to ourselves in fear of losing ourselves. Indeed, we feel free to lose ourselves in the loving arms of the other.

What finds its climax in orgasm happens in every love. When we love another person we dedicate ourselves to her or him. We don't want to hold onto ourselves. We want to be with our loved one. We want to dedicate ourselves to the other because this person means everything to us. This kind of dedication allows us to experience a new kind of wealth in our life. When we dedicate ourselves to another person we receive such a bounty of gifts that we feel richer, more alive and freer than ever before. But often we feel unable to dedicate ourselves to another person. We are mistrusting, afraid that our dedication might be abused, that we may lose ourselves. We become especially incapable of dedication when we have a need to control everything around us, including our emotions, our relationships, our words and actions, in fear of making a mistake or embarrassing ourselves. But then we lack an essential part of successful living. When we cannot dedicate ourselves completely to something outside of ourselves we will ultimately remain lonely. We cannot really encounter another person. Without the dedication of full self-giving we cannot love and we cannot live.

Many stories tell of saints who have given themselves wholly to God. They put themselves at his disposal. They prayed that God would use them for whatever God wanted them. We find it difficult to pray such a prayer of utter self-giving. But in such self-giving the saints became free. They could go forward full of confidence in the future. They knew that whatever God planned for them would ultimately be good. The prayer of St. Nicholas of Flüe, who died in 1487, is famous: "O my God, and my Lord, take me away from me/ And give me wholly to Thee." This prayer turned Nicholas into a mystic, and made him completely transparent to the reality beyond our reality. Thus he could become a peacemaker for his contemporaries. He became an angel who showed his country a new way, because he knew to keep himself out of the conflicts, and he looked at everything from God's perspective.

But dedication does not mean to abandon ourselves; it means to find ourselves anew in the Divine. Jesus said that such dedication is the prerequisite for us to bring forth fruit. Though at times in fact we use religious activity to hang on tightly to ourselves, to our safety and our salvation. But that will make our live barren. This way we cannot experience the richness and life that can come only from self-giving.

May the Angel of Dedication teach you the art of fully devoting yourself to your work, to the people you love, and to the One who is the source of love. Dedication will richly reward you. It leads you to freedom and into an unfathomable confidence that your life will be fine. May you be able to let go of yourself. May you feel that you are carried. May your defenses dissolve. Then you feel alive and wide open. Then your life will become fruitful. When you dedicate yourself to something other than yourself you will flourish; devoting yourself you will flourish.

THE ANGEL OF HARMONY

PSYCHOLOGISTS DISLIKE THE WORD 'harmonize.' Where we cannot stand up to conflict or bear differences of opinion, we want to sweep all disagreements under the carpet for harmony's sake. We create artificial harmony, which halts progress. The problems go on festering and eventually break out again. This kind of false harmony comes from our fear of the truth. We cannot stand quarreling. Maybe it reminds us of seeing our parents quarrel when we were little children. We were frightened that they might leave us alone and we might lose their protection. Conflict throughout our lives might stir in us an existential fear that the floor will drop from under our feet. We harmonize, pretending that there is no discord, that really everyone is right. Or worse, we harmonize by incessantly moralizing, for example with the argument that we are all Christians and ought to be loving with each other.

184

The Angel of Harmony does not want you "to harmonize" but calls you to the art of coming into harmony within yourself, of agreeing to yourself and of living in tune with yourself. The Greek word *harmozein* means to put together. You attain inner harmony when you compose all that is conflicting within yourself. You become aware of your contradictions and allow them, so they no longer tear you apart. You bring order, and allow each part of you its own tenor. Then everything resounds in harmony. You are in tune with all that is within you. You need not repress anything or exclude anything from the harmony. All that is in you is allowed to resonate — for whenever you suppress parts of yourself, for example your rage or your fear, they will be missing from your soul's accord, and no true harmony can come into existence.

When we are in tune with ourselves, we can create harmony around us. Not the kind of artificial harmony rising from conciliating. This means a bringing together of different opinions and disagreements and of the people who stand for these different points of view. Then nothing gets swept under the carpet. All different viewpoints are looked at and defined ever more clearly. All points of view are respected and not immediately judged. Every opinion is heard and can be openly discussed with others. Problems are talked through until everything is sorted out, until a solution is found that everybody can live with, one that does not break up other people's harmony. Then we do not artificially harmonize but find ways in which we can go forward together despite our differences.

As people of harmony we will create surroundings where others enjoy being and working. There discords are followed by restored harmony. When we are in tune with ourselves, we do not need intrigues aiming to turn colleagues against one another. Rather we create an atmosphere of clarity and concord where everyone can feel respected. Then all can play their part in the great symphony of the company or the community. My wish for you is that the Angel of Harmony transform you to become yourself an Angel of Harmony, so that others around you will find the courage to sound their own uniquely personal note.

THE ANGEL OF CLARITY

Y OU MAY REMEMBER A DISCUSSION when someone stated with great clarity what the issues were, listened to all arguments, seemed to sense the emotions present, and was able to express essential questions and clearly point towards a solution. Or it was in a personal conversation when you were able to tell someone quite clearly what was being overlooked, where blockages sat, and what you needed to change, so that things could get better. We may never have learned this formally nor studied psychology, but there was a clear sense of what was going on. When thus clear we may speak little, but when we do we hit the nail on the head. We are able to clear up something that was murky and opaque. We are then Angels of Clarity for others. They are like the angels painted by Filippo Lippi, whose faces reflect a bright transparent clarity.

But the Angel of Clarity also calls you to bring out the talents that lie dormant within you. Surely, you have had the experience of suddenly seeing something very plainly, that all at once you understood. This was for the people of times before ours the mystery of enlightenment, to suddenly see everything with clarity. Not to notice particulars, but in the twinkling of an eye to see everything becoming clear. At that moment we can say yes to our life — we feel that everything is alright. We do not spot anything concrete, but we find ourselves getting a glimpse into a depth so deep that things clear up. This kind of experience is always a gift, a gift that clarifies everything, one that allows what is essential to shine through the shadows of things. Then we touch true being and the principal and undistorted image of our true self.

You might also remember an experience when all of a sudden you knew exactly what to do, what was your mission in life, which path to take. Suddenly you recognize who you are. You may have spent a long time reflecting on your life and seemingly going nowhere. But as if from heaven came a flash of light at once illuminating your entire life. That was the Angel of Clarity calling upon you and opening your eyes to the core. We may have to make a decision and for a long while are unsure what to decide. There are so many arguments for and against. There are so many possibilities to choose from, for example when deciding on a new career path. But when the Angel of Clarity touches us we become clear about our direction. We can feel the Angel rearranging our divided heart. We may have gotten ourselves into a messy situation, and cannot see the ins and outs anymore. But suddenly everything clears up, and once again we feel the presence of the Angel.

The Angel of Clarity wishes to help you to know yourself clearly, and to behold your own depths. Once you are experienced you yourself may become an Angel of Clarity to

others. In talking you may clearly see what others need and what would help them. You can bring order to their muddled thoughts. People will be grateful to you. One cannot just learn to be clear. We need the Angel of Clarity to initiate us. We can pray that the

Angel of Clarity will come help us when a friend is in a difficult situation and wants to talk. The Angel of Clarity allows you to go into the conversation without the pressure to succeed or miraculously resolve all of your friend's problems. You can be relaxed, because you trust that the Angel of Clarity will come to your aid and empower you to find the clarity and help needed. Perhaps you won't be able to say anything for a long while, because you do not have a clear understanding. But all at once you may feel a slight impulse. You say something, and it resonates. Then you know that the Angel of Clarity has been with you.

THE ANGEL OF SLOWNESS

66 "THE DEVIL INVENTED HASTE," says a Turkish proverb. We speak of 'heavenly peace.' The Angel of Slowness calls us to remember this attribute of Paradise. The novel *The Discovery of Slowness* has become a cult book. Obviously the author, Sten Nadolny, touched a nerve and a deep yearning of our day. Not only are our nerves often raw from constant stress, but our hectic lifestyle damages our souls and we suffer from the pressures of the relentless economy of time. When everything has to keep going more quickly, when not a moment can be wasted at work, when there are no more breaks, and everything speeds ever faster, we need an antidote: the discovery of slowness. There is so much we could rediscover when quiet and slow. Rather than speeding up, we need to slow down.

When we watch a panther in a cage, we marvel at its slow, majestic movements. We know that in the very next moment it could pounce with lightning speed upon its prey. Yet it has time, it allows itself time. For us, though, time is money. We must save as much time as possible, so that we have free time for more important things. The question then is: what is more important to us? Often we cannot do much at all with all that time saved. We are habitually in a rush. But where to? We've become the victims of our own frenzy — we rush at all times, including in our free time. Here, too, we want to do ever more ever faster. But this constant rushing takes away our ability to feel and to experience the things we do. Increasingly, we only feel alive in the midst of the hustles and bustles. But life itself, we no longer feel. We no longer feel ourselves, our breathing, our body, or the stirrings of our heart. "Idleness is the beginning of all love," the poet Ingeborg Bachman once said.

We can practice this idling in our daily activities. Walk slowly, become aware of every step, let nothing push you — nothing — and you will arrive in your presence leading you to intense experience and inner peace. Slowness has its own beauty. When we slowly stroll along a street, people take notice of us; they can feel that we enjoy our walk. When we rush past the stores, we are only thinking of our destination, we are not on the way, not really in our body; and we lose the ability to enjoy and celebrate ourselves in that moment. To the ancient Greek Stoic philosophers our life is an ongoing celebration. We celebrate that we are human, yet ours is a divine dignity. Something of this celebration can be felt in the slowness of our movements. We walk slowly; we handle things slowly. We leave ourselves time for conversation. We leave ourselves time to eat. We eat slowly and with awareness. And suddenly we notice how good the food tastes. We savor it. Surely, it can be a feast to chew one piece of bread slowly.

The Angel of Slowness calls you to the art of being, the experience of living intensely. Try it some time. Walk slowly from one cubicle to the next. When you go out for a walk, feel every step you take, feel how you tread upon the earth and lift up your feet again. Pick up your cup slowly and hold it in your hand. At night change into your pajamas slowly; put your daytime clothes away as a symbol of putting way the day's worries. You will find that everything becomes a symbol when you move slowly. In the morning try to wash slowly, enjoying the cold water that refreshes you. Then get dressed slowly. The liturgy of the Catholic mass provides for this slow dressing. When the priest puts on the Mass vestments he says, "I put on the garments of salvation." Likewise, you can consciously be glad of the clothes you put on as you dress yourself in them and prepare to meet the day. You can thank God with the words of Psalm 139: "I praise you because you have formed me so wonderfully" (v. 14). The Angel of Slowness wants to lead you to live with attentive awareness and teach you the art of making your life an enduring celebration.

THE ANGEL OF RETREAT

IN THE FOURTH CENTURY Christian monks started a great movement of retreat. They had had enough of the noisiness of the world and were disappointed that the Church itself was becoming worldly. Many retreated to the desert to live by themselves, apart from the world. They wanted to contemplate their own truth and follow their deepest desire, experiencing God in prayer and becoming one with God. It is surprising that precisely those who withdrew from the world came to have a most profound impact on that world. Crowds of pilgrims and people seeking help set out from Rome and Athens for the deserts of Egypt, in order to get advice from the Desert Fathers, as these monks came to be called. These pilgrims apparently felt that these monks who had the courage to retreat and to face their truth before God knew more about being human than the philosophers and doctors who lived amid the hustle and bustle of the world.

From time to time we all need to retreat from the noise and rush of daily life. Otherwise things overwhelm us. We function but no longer are we really living or being ourselves. When you retreat to a silent place you may take all the noise of your world along; you may not find it very pleasant to face all the things that surface in you. It requires some time for you to free yourself from the problems of your everyday. Only then begins the inner retreat. You withdraw, you step back from what you are doing and what you are involved in. You get in touch with yourself and discover what matters at the bottom of your heart. You recognize your deeper truth. This can be painful. But when you look at yourself truly and hold yourself out to God, who accepts you as you are, you feel inner freedom and peace. You understand that you are unique and irreplacable. You comprehend that you are valuable and important, because you can make a unique impression on this world, which no one else can. And you just may discover the inner fountain that bubbles up inside you and never fails, because it is a divine spring, the spring of the Spirit.

The Angel of Retreat encourages you to retreat even from your spouse or partner at times. When we are constantly with another person, we begin to feel trapped. We hang on each other, and that is not good for any relationship. We need space and freedom between us, so that we can breathe and bring to the union our own special qualities. Our spouse or partner may bitterly reproach us for retreating. But I have met many people who have retreated and have found that it benefited their lives together. Taking time for ourselves helps us to become our whole self again. It is like visiting a spa where we'd recover our own resources. Then our life with each other will regain its sparkle. We can develop a new imagination and enjoyment in our relationship with our spouse or partner. When we retreat, we can appreciate that we cannot define ourselves only by our partner. We need something deeper; we need our own source of life that is God who made us each a unique human person. So my wish for you is that the Angel of Retreat may show you when it is time to retreat again. I wish that then you will find you are not alone, because the Angel of Retreat is with you, revealing a new horizon to your future lifc.

THE ANGEL
OF MINDFULNESS

THE ANGEL OF MINDFULNESS is related to the Angel of Slowness. Today mindfulness is a favorite word used by spiritual writers. In particular the Vietnamese Buddhist monk Thich Nhat Hanh often speaks about mindfulness and the art of living mindfully. For him this is the whole wisdom of Buddhism, to let the energy of mindfulness flow into every single daily activity. Even as a young monk he learned to perform all his everyday tasks mindfully. His whole ascetic practice and daily training consisted in being mindful of everything — of his breathing, walking, washing dishes, and washing his hands. Every time he washed his hands he said, "Water flows over these hands. May I use it carefully to preserve our precious planet."

The word 'mindfulness' expresses respect, observation, esteem, and notice. It is connected with being awake. When we give mindful respect to our breathing, mindfully measure our step, mindfully pick up a spoon, when we are wholly involved in what we are doing at the moment, we are awake. The Buddha is called the Awakened One. But we can spend our whole life asleep. Then we do not notice what we are doing. We have illusions about our life. We are not in touch with reality. Mindfulness offers to bring us in touch with things and people. A Zen monk was once asked about his practice of meditation. He answered, "When I eat, I am eating. When I sit, I am sitting. When I stand, I am standing. When I walk, I am walking." The questioner said, "There is nothing special about that. We all do it." The monk replied: "No, when you sit, you are already standing up and when you stand up, you are already on your way."

The practice of meditation consists simply in this — paying attention to what you are doing at the moment. Then you will realize that attentiveness is a spiritual power that infuses your life with a new spice. You will feel that you yourself are living, rather than being lived. You will feel that life is a mystery, full of depth, full of vitality, and full of joy.

Mindfulness has to do with the respect and the esteem of things. I treat my breathing with respect, because in it I feel God's breath filling me with life, penetrating my whole body with its healing warmth. Respectfully, I pick up the tool I am going to use, because I see the care that has been put into making it. I treat the flowers in my room with high regard, because in them I feel the mystery of creation and the Creator himself.

Not only for Zen monks, but also for Western monks, mindfulness is the mark of a spiritual person. St. Benedict told his monks to treat the monastery's equipment and tools with care and respect, because everything is precious; everything is a sacred altar vessel. However, even we monks forget to be mindful. Too often we go about our books unconsciously and use cutlery or handle tools without awareness. Too often we bang the door unconsciously. So in our daily unawareness and inattentiveness we all need the Angel of Mindfulness to keep in touch with ourselves, to wake us from slumber, and to make us live mindfully, wholly in the present moment, giving all our attention to what we are doing at the very moment.

Being mindful in everything gives our lives a gentle breathing. Then we are wholly in the present, wholly at one with ourselves and the world. But mindfulness is not automatic. You have to practice it every day. It becomes the measure of your spirituality. However many pious words I speak, however many spiritual talks I give, without mindfulness they are all hot air. My wish for you is that the Angel of Mindfulness may lead you ever deeper into the art of living, so that you discover the joy of living and may do everything with mindfulness and respect, because everything is precious, everything is wonderfully created by God and filled with soul by His Spirit.

THE ANGEL OF MILDNESS

F OR ME THE MILD AUTUMN LIGHT is an image for myself looking mildly at myself, my faults and weaknesses, but also at others and their human failings. With this mild gaze we can bathe our own reality and that of others in a mild glow. In the mild autumn light everything looks beautiful. The colorful leaves on a tree shine in all their beauty. Even the withered tree appears beautiful. Everything gets its own shine. I have seen old people beaming out a mildness of this kind. I like to be near them. I like talking to them. They make me feel that I can be who I am; they communicate "Everything is good." Life surely can buffet people this way and that. As we age, we have had our ups and downs. But now in the autumn of life we may look at everything with a mild gaze. Nothing human is alien to us. We do not judge. We let life shine in the mild autumn light, just as it is.

The medieval word 'mild' comes from 'mill.' So 'mild' means milled, ground up fine, tender, soft, or mellow. We are not mild by nature. Mildness requires the grinding process. Only then does the hard corn become soft and mealy. The word 'mealy' comes from *mola*, meaning millstone. Mild old people have been ground in the mill of life. They have been through crises, they have known despair. They have been through dark valleys. They have battled with their faults and weaknesses

and have often lost the battle. But they have always stood up again and fought on. The millstone of their life has ground them soft. They have not rebelled against this millstone. They said yes to it grinding them up. So they have become mild. Perhaps you have experienced the angel described by the early 20th century poet Werner Bergengruen in his Angel Prayer:

Brother Angel, every night,
before demons could undo me,
You, O Guardian, with your wings
have kindled blushing morning light.

You have borne me like a brother
through the fiery depths of hell,
Hewed out steps where feet might tread
on the cliff face sheer and tall,
Shielded me from rope and bullet,
Blasted walls for me to pass.
Though I've often been a burden,
Always have you kept your faith.
On these roads of murky shadow,
You, my Angel, guard my side,
Thanklessly and without welcome.
Angel, seize me out of time!
Just once more, O Angel, lead me
where you will, then you shall fly.
From my chest lift off the stone.
Angel, leave me not alone.

Clearly the poet felt that the Angel of Mildness had carried him through hells and abysses, grinding him in the mill and making him mild.

Mildness and gentleness belong together. For the writer monk Evagrius Ponticus, gentleness is the mark of the spiritual person.

The kind of ascetic practice that makes you hard and self-righteous is worthless. Only gentle people like David and Jesus have understood the spiritual way. When we judge others harshly we have not yet overcome our own faults and weaknesses. We may have only repressed them. We may have fought against them violently, and now we attack others with the same violence. Then we project our repressed passions onto others. We have not been through the mill of truth. We have not yet become soft and tender.

My wish for you is that you may meet many an Angel of Mildness in your life. You will feel how people like this do you good. Perhaps you already know some of these mild people. Seek them out, talk to them, ask them how they became the way they are. Then you can learn from them how to look mildly and bathe your life in mild autumn light, which lends everything in you its own dignity and beauty — even your failures. When you have been to this school of the mild, perhaps you too will be able to become an Angel of Mildness for other people, who rage against themselves, judge themselves harshly, and despair at their own shortcomings. You do not need to say very much to them. Perhaps they will feel from your mild gaze that they too can see their life in another light, not in a harsh condemning spotlight, but bathed in the mild soft light of autumn.

THE ANGEL OF HUMILITY

THE OLD GERMANIC PEOPLE translated the Latin word *humilitas* in their own way as 'serving.' In the world of knightly allegiance, to serve meant being someone's servant or runner. Humility then meant to run for someone else, having the courage to serve, the courage to serve life and to stand up for others. This requires a readiness to set oneself aside, to become free of oneself in order to risk oneself for others. But this interpretation covers just one aspect of the biblical idea of humility.

The Latin word *humilitas* comes from *humus*, meaning earth or soil. Humilitas then means the courage to accept our own earthiness, the courage to reconcile ourselves with the truth that we are from the earth, that we are flesh and blood people, with instincts and vital needs. Those who do not have this courage to look at the truth about themselves are blind. Perhaps this is the meaning of the famous story of the healing of the man born blind, found in the gospel of John (John 9). Jesus heals him by spitting on the ground, the earth, humus, and mixing the spit with earth into a mud paste. He smears this dirt onto the blind man's eyes and, by reconnecting him to the earth, heals him.

For monks, humility, meaning the courage to face the truth about oneself, is the sign of genuine spirituality. When we are proud of our spiritual life and set ourselves above others who give way to their moods and instincts, we have not yet come face to face with the truth about ourselves. The writer Herman Hesse describes this in a fascinating way in his book *Siddhartha*. At first Siddhartha practices severe asceticism, but he fails. Then he goes out into the world and gives free rein to all his desires. Finally, he becomes sated with this life and he returns. At the river he suddenly receives his great enlightenment. He sees the "child people" crossing the river in a boat. Earlier on, he would have set himself above them. Now he empathizes with them. He feels a deep oneness with them. He is just like them. He feels compassion for them but also hope. He judges no one but he knows that for all people what counts is the greater love that can transform everything. The Angel of Humility took him into the school of enlightenment and taught him that he can experience oneness with other people and himself only if he is

215

prepared to come down to them and to his own truth.

Humble people are not people who belittle themselves, who shirk all the things they should do, because they do not trust themselves. When humble we are not hunchbacks who demean ourselves in false submission. When humble we become people who have the courage to face the truth about ourselves, and so behave modestly. Then we know that all this world's abysses are also within us, and we do not judge others. Then, because we have bent down and faced our own earthiness, we can become Angels of Humility, who can set others up on their feet when they fail.

Humilitas is also connected with humor. As humble people we are humorous. We can laugh about ourselves. We can stand back and look at ourselves calmly, because we have allowed ourselves to be as we are, human beings of earth and heaven, human beings with faults and weaknesses, who are also lovable and precious. My wish for you is that the Angel of Humility give you the courage to accept and love yourself in your own earthiness and humanity. Then you will give out hope and confidence to everyone you meet. The Angel of Humility will create a space around you, in which people find the courage to step down into their own reality and thereby step up into true life.

THE ANGEL
OF FULFILLMENT

THE WORD 'FULFILLMENT' can have various meanings. We long for our wishes and desires to be fulfilled. We also know that no human being can fulfill our deepest yearnings. When we love someone we feel completely filled with this love. Yet at the same time there grows a longing within us for an unconditional love, unconditional safety, and unconditional support. No earthly human being can give us anything unconditional. From time immemorial, as humans we have called upon angels to help us when we want our desires to be fulfilled. We have felt that we cannot fulfill everything by ourselves. Of course we can fulfill our wishes for a new dress or a new car, if we have enough money in our checking account. But we need the Angel of Fulfillment to help us if we wish for a successful friendship, good health, or a job that suits us. The fulfillment of these wishes depends on higher powers beyond our control. Then we ask that our Angel stand by us and grant our heart's desire.

To fulfill also means to do something and to finish it. The Angel of Fulfillment wants to strengthen you to complete what you take on. It does you no good if you only go halfway, if you only begin something and do not finish it. This is true of household repairs. Nothing is worse than a half-decorated room that is never finished. It would also be true for a letter to your friend that you have begun. A letter that is unfinished just annoys you. Then you need the Angel of Fulfillment to give you strength and perseverance to finish what you've started. Only then can you move to the next project with new energy. Things you have begun but not finished discourage you. You cannot live on bits and pieces. You long for some things to be completely done.

Completion is another meaning of the word 'fulfill.' The Greek word for completion is telos. It means goal, the whole, completion, and perfection. The gospel of John frequently uses this word for the love of Jesus Christ. "Having loved his own who were in the world, he loved them to the end" (John 13:1). As he is dying on the cross he says: "It is finished" (John 19:39). This saying recalls the words used by the ancient mystery cults when concluding their hallowed rituals. Here completion means initiation into God's mystery. God alone is complete and perfect. When we say people have lived a full life, that they are fulfilled and complete, we also mean that they share in God's fullness, in the completion that God alone can give. The Angel of Fulfillment would like to lead you into the mystery of completion and thereby into the mystery of God. In everything you complete there shines something of the completion that is in God. You get an inkling of your life becoming whole. Sometimes, perhaps you have the impression that your life is only bits and pieces, which you cannot put together. The Jewish mystics have found precisely in their faith the attempt to find meaning in their suffering: "Only a broken heart is a whole heart." The Angel of Fulfillment wants to show you that the many bits and pieces of your life fit together and that they make up a perfect whole. Your life can become healed, fulfilled, and complete. You are no longer torn in all directions by contradictory wishes and needs. You are whole. You are fulfilled. The Angel of Fulfillment brings back together what is torn apart in you and completes what is in fragments. It fulfills your deepest yearning to be one, to be whole.

THE ANGEL OF ENDURANCE

AT THE BEGINNING of a new year, a week, or even a day, many of us make resolutions. We may be enthusiastic about a book we read and, accordingly, want to change our lives all at once. Or we heard a talk on time management or problem solving. So we set out to work with fervor. Yet after a short while we run out of steam. Things become too difficult, and we give up. Suddenly it is no longer fun to work on ourselves, particularly when there is nothing to show for it. It appears worthless. We feel that we'll never get anywhere anyway. But by giving up our resolution, we are giving up a piece of ourselves. We no longer trust ourselves. We resign. And gradually a sense of futility slips in. It all seems meaningless. Things will stay the same anyway. I cannot change myself. I cannot make myself better. Poemen, one of the early Desert Fathers, said to a young monk who was filled with such thoughts of resigning: "What is the point of applying yourself to a craft and not learning it properly?" Learn the craft of becoming a human being and stop moaning!

The Angel of Endurance would like to lead you to stick to your resolutions. As the proverb says: "The road to hell is paved with good intentions." If you keep planning things and never carry them through, you are preparing a hell for yourself here and now. Your life will become a hell of self-reproaches and self-criticism, which will devour you. Without endurance your life has no constancy. The word 'endure' comes from *durare*, meaning to last, to remain, to be constant, and to stick it out. If you

go to work without endurance you never stand firm. You flap around and nibble at things. But nothing develops. Something can grow only if it can take root. Jesus himself compares people without endurance to the stony ground on which the word of God falls: "They have no root in themselves, but are inconsistent; then when trouble or persecution arises … immediately they fall away" (Mark 4:17). As soon as things get difficult, as soon as we feel any resistance, we give up. Gradually this makes us not take anything on in the first place.

Reflect on where you will next need the Angel of Endurance. Perhaps it is at work, where not everything is going as you would wish. When you stick at it, when you don't give up, when you don't just tell yourself there is nothing to be done, you will see that the situation at your work place can change. Or perhaps you are working on one of your weaknesses. You think you have so often planned to learn to control your anger or deal with your eating problem. But nothing has worked. First, set yourself realistic goals and do not chase after illusions. See what you really can change and what is simply your character, with which you must come to terms. But when you undertake to change something in yourself, stick to it. If you do not succeed, ask yourself whether you went about it in the wrong way or took on too much. Then set yourself a more modest goal. But stick to it, and you will find your endurance is rewarded. The Angel of Endurance will give you the feeling that it is possible to change something in yourself; it is enjoyable if you stick to it with endurance. You are not simply a prey to circumstances. You can do something. Trust that you are not alone. When you want to give in, look about you! Then you will see the Angel of Endurance standing beside you. The Angel will not leave you until your life acquires a firm foundation, one that is constant and enduring.

THE ANGEL OF TRUST

AGAIN AND AGAIN I HEAR THIS: "I can't trust anyone. I didn't learn to trust as a child. My trust has so often been abused. So with the best will in the world I can't manage to trust anyone." But we are lonely that way and will remain so. We may not trust ourselves to open up to another person, because we are afraid of being let down again. Neither do we trust another person's love. Immediately doubt comes: "He only loves me because he feels sorry for me, or because he wants something from me, or wants to use me for his own ends." It does not help to say, "You just have to trust people!" All of us want to trust others, but some of us can't. The reason usually lies in our childhood. We had no choice about it. There are others among us who experienced their parents as reliable; they are able not only to trust their parents but also others. They approach people with trust. They have a basic trust in life, in things, in God, so they can be daring. They take risks because they trust that things will be alright.

If I wish you the Angel of Trust, I trust you are not at the mercy of the mistrust you acquired as a child. You can learn to trust. You can go to school with the Angel of Trust. But you can't just decide that from today on you will trust people. Trust has to grow. You need some positive experiences of other people, people who prove themselves to be reliable and trustworthy. But you also need to be prepared to trust what people offer you. If you regard your friends with distrust, they have no chance to prove you can trust them. You will take everything they say and do in a negative way. So at least you have to give trust a try. How do you do this? You can pretend as if another person is worthy of your trust. You can see how you feel when you take everything a friend says as genuine, if you completely trust this person. Of course a few doubts will slip in. Reserve these doubts for later. Just try to trust your friend for at least a week. You will see how this does you good, and how it proves increasingly right to trust this person.

Of course you always take a risk when you trust someone. You have no guarantee that your trust is justified. It helps me to know that I am supported at a deeper level. I know I am supported by a higher power. Even when a human being does abuse my trust, I trust God, who holds me in his loving hands. This trust in God prevents me from falling into a slough of depression when someone abuses my trust.

For all of human history we have trusted that a guardian angel accompanies us. We can call upon our guardian angels, not only in the midst of dangerous traffic, but also when we are unsure whether to trust someone. My wish for you is that you may always be aware you are accompanied by the Angel of Trust. Then you do not have to be 100 percent certain whether you can trust this or that person at any given moment. You do not have to lose your trust even when someone disappoints you. The Angel of Trust will stay with you and keep renewing your courage to trust yourself and to risk trusting others. This is what trust means, relying on something over which you do not have power.

Because such daring is an essential part of trust, it is good to know that an Angel of Trust is beside us. The Angel has contact with what is beyond our power. At a deeper level, the Angel of Trust gives us the trust we need in our dealings with people: the trust that can never be completely destroyed by other people, because that is not within their power either.

This trust gives us freedom to keep going back to people with trust. It makes us able to be daring, to take risks. "Who dares, wins," says the proverb. When we want to control all things so that they will succeed, life will slip between our fingers. The Angel of Trust wants to initiate you more deeply into trusting life and trusting others. You will realize that you are not determined by the lack of

trust you learned as a child. An Angel wants
to set your trust on a firm foundation, upon
which you can build your life.

THE ANGEL OF COMPASSION

WE ARE COMPASSIONATE when we have a heart for the poor, the orphaned, the unfortunate, and the lonely. But before we can have a heart for the poor, we must first have a heart for what is poor and unhappy in ourselves. We must learn first to be compassionate with ourselves. The Latin *misericordia* means mercy or compassion, having a heart for the unhappy and unfortunate. In the Jewish tradition when speaking of mercy or compassion, one thinks of a mother's womb. The compassionate God carries us lovingly in the divine womb. Like a mother, God can wait until we grow into the image in which He has made us. When Jesus has compassion for people, the Bible often uses the Greek word *splanchnizomai* which means "to be gripped in the guts." For the Greeks the guts or intestines were the seat of sensitive feelings. To be compassionate means letting someone else touch the place where I am sensitive. The Bible has yet another word for mercy or compassion: *eleos*, meaning tenderness, sympathy, and pity.

So being compassionate toward ourselves means treating ourselves well and with tenderness, not raging against ourselves, not making too many demands on ourselves, but simply having a heart for ourselves, just as we have become — having a heart for what is weak and orphaned in ourselves. We often treat ourselves mercilessly. We judge ourselves when we make a mistake. We scold ourselves when something goes wrong. We have a ruthless critic inside ourselves, a hardhearted superego, who judges all our thoughts and feelings, who punishes us if we do not fulfill its demands. And often we cannot cope with this ruthless superego. We need the words of Jesus, who shows us the merciful Father who does not reject the prodigal son but makes a feast for him, because he who was lost has been found, he who was dead has returned to life. We need an Angel of Compassion to take the power away from our inner judges and fill our hearts with compassionate love. It is not enough to decide to be compassionate with your mind and will. A ruthless superego lodges in your unconscious. In order to overcome it you need the Angel of Compassion.

When we treat ourselves with compassion, we can also learn compassion toward others. I know people who are compassionate toward the sick and lonely, but who are completely ruthless toward themselves. There is a place in their heart for everyone else but none for themselves. They force themselves to repress all their own needs in order to be there for others. But a

lack of compassion for ourselves may distort the help we give to others. A kind of possessiveness can slip into our love. We may get annoyed when our exaggerated love is not honored. In order to love another person from the heart, in order really to have a heart for another, we must first get in touch with our own heart; we must feel with our heart for all that is poor and unhappy in ourselves. Then can we be compassionate. Then we will not condemn others, but embrace them, along with all that is unhappy, broken, and unattractive in their heart. Then our help will not give another a bad conscience. But this person can find a place, a home in our heart. My wish for you is that the Angel of Compassion will teach you to open your heart to what is poor in yourself and others. Then your heart will become like a womb, in which you yourself and others can grow. Then people around you will also be able to get in touch with their own hearts and cease condemning themselves ruthlessly. "Anyone who has a heart can be saved," said one of the fourth-century Church Fathers. If you have a heart for the poor and weak, your life will succeed. Then the Angel in you will rejoice over the compassion that dwells in your heart.

THE ANGEL
OF CONSOLATION

WHENEVER WE EXPERIENCE LOSS we need consolation and comfort: when a friendship breaks up, when someone hurts us deeply, or when a loved one passes away in death. Consolation encompasses different kinds of experience, as language reveals. The English word 'trust' is used in German as *Trost*, meaning consolation, and faithfulness and steadfastness as well. When we suffer a loss, we lose our balance. Then we need someone to restore our strength, our steadfastness. The Greek Bible's word for comfort is *parakalein*. It means to summon, invite, appeal for help, encourage, and speak words of consolation. When we experience a lack or loss we need an angel to stand beside us, to support us when we need it, and to speak words of comfort. It is above all this offering of comforting words that the ancient Greeks associated with consolation: words that give meaning to the senselessness that all loss causes. But words must not be platitudes that fail to connect with people. When we speak platitudes, we do not comfort others, we speak past them. We merely say something we are not really convinced of ourselves. We utter words that offer no support and make no sense of the loss. We speak in hackneyed empty phrases. But to console means to find words that connect heart to heart, words that come truly from the heart. Such words touch others' hearts, open up a new horizon before them, and offer some firm ground to stand on.

The Latin word for consolation is *consolari*. Ultimately, it means to be with people who are alone, who have been left alone with their pain, their loss, and their need. To console then means to visit others when they are closed up in themselves, when need and pain have locked their mouths and hearts. Not everyone can do this. Often we do not have the courage to knock at the door of a person barricaded behind their pain. We may not find the courage to go into a house of mourning and meet the mourner's bottomless neediness and loneliness. Being with those who suffer also means sharing their pain and staying with them in their pain. We cannot console others from the outside, by mouthing pious words we read somewhere else. We have enter their space. We must enter their house of darkness, devastation, and suffering. When you are able to go into their house of mourning, the mourning person will experience you as an Angel of Consolation. He or she will feel that through you, the angel of God has visited him like a "dawning from on high" (Luke 1:78).

Throughout our history as humans in our pain we have appealed to the Angel of Consolation to visit and stay with us. The composer Johann Sebastian Bach expressed this movingly in the tenor aria for his Michaelmas cantata: "Stay, you Angels, stay with me! Guideth me on either side, that my feet may never faulter!" It is a fervent song conveying the confidence that we shall not be left alone with our suffering, but that God's angels accompany us, remain at our sides, and endure until our pain has been transformed into a song of thanksgiving. My wish for you is that an Angel may comfort you when you are sad. May this Angel set you firmly on your feet when you stumble, speak to you when you have become speechless with pain, visit you in your loneliness, and make you feel that you are no longer alone. Then you know that an Angel stands beside you and will go with you all the way. When you know of the Angel of Comfort, you can face your sadness and be comforted. You need not brush over it. When in sadness you are deeply consoled, this sadness will no longer weaken you but lead you deeper into the mystery of your own self and, if you so believe, the mystery of Jesus Christ, who has come down into our human mourning becoming "consolation for the whole world."

THE ANGEL OF PRUDENCE

PRUDENCE IS THE FIRST of the four cardinal virtues. It is the capacity to discover what is appropriate and beneficial for me here and now. The Latin word *prudentia* comes from *providentia* and means foresight, caution. When we are prudent we look out and around. We behave with care. We see beyond what is right under our noses. We have a wider horizon. We discern reality and see things as they are. For the Greek philosopher Aristotle, prudence is the precondition for all the other virtues. First of all, we need to see reality correctly. Then we can behave appropriately. According to the philosopher Josef Pieper, this virtue "enables us to be and to do what we are here for." Our lives will only be empowered when we behave in accordance with our own reality. The ancients distinguished prudence from wisdom. Wisdom knows the mystery of being, whereas prudence sees how to apply this knowledge of reality to each moment and convert it into practical living.

You need the Angel of Prudence when you have to make a decision. The Angel of Prudence sees further than you and has a wider horizon. This angel foresees what consequences your decision might have. Ask your Angel of Prudence to help you discern the deepest motives for your decisions and which decision fits the reality best. You need the Angel of Prudence when you have to judge a situation or are asked to sort out a dispute. At times we may be over-eager and think that love is all we need. We think that love will resolve everything. But when we are prudent we look at a situation carefully. We seek for the causes of the conflict. We listen to different opinions. Only when we have heard it all and thought it over do we offer a conclusion, and one that seeks for ways to settle the dispute. A prudent person sees everything and tries to understand everything in order to be able to judge rightly.

Jesus calls prudent those who have built their house upon a rock. When we build our house on rock we do not behave with undue haste. We then do not build on the sand of our illusions, or the sand of our enthusiasm, but on the rock of a solid life, as Jesus preached in his Sermon on the Mount. When prudent we weigh everything. We act with consideration. We understand what is at stake. This doesn't mean that we are know-it-alls but that we know what is essential and think about it carefully. The prudent person finds the solution appropriate to the moment. The prudent virgins, who brought oil for their lamps so that they could endure a long wait and be ready when the wedding feast began (Matthew 25), looked ahead. They looked beyond the moment and thought of the future. The foolish virgins lived only for the moment. Prudence is clearly necessary for our lives to succeed.

Klug, the German word for prudence, means fine, tender, delicate, cultured, intellectually agile, courageous, and brave. Prudent people think not only with their minds but also with their hearts. When prudent, we bravely seize the opportunities offered us. We see the fine distinctions, which cruder minds would overlook. Prudence is practical reason, knowledge converted into action, in accordance with reality. Great knowledge helps little if you do not know what is right for the here and now. I wish you the Angel of Prudence, so that at every moment you may recognize the path that leads you on. May this Angel take you further and guide you into greater freedom, breadth of vision, and love.

THE ANGEL OF REVERENCE

THE GERMAN WORD FOR REVERENCE is *Ehrfurcht*, from the words for honor (Ehre) and fear (Furcht). In this case the fear is not fear of other people or dangerous situations, but awe. It means not to push yourself forward but to keep the appropriate distance. Reverence originates in the religious realm. "It is the awareness of the unapproachably holy, which in early human consciousness surrounded everything that was high, mighty, and wonderful" (Romano Guardini, a philosopher of religion). When we are reverent we do not take possession of what we marvel at. We stand back in awe. We show the necessary respect for other people, for creation, and for what we admire. We do not insist on penetrating a person's mystery. We let the mystery be. Guardini also holds that all true culture begins with people standing back and allowing people their dignity, and works their beauty. True culture requires reverence. In all religions angels communicate the feeling of reverence. They bring something from beyond into our lives, something that matters greatly to us, something that transcends us, from which we can only stand back in awe.

Out of reverence, we curb our curiosity about people and do not probe their intimate secrets. For St. Benedict, reverence ultimately means that we believe in the good core of other people, that we see in others

the divine spark, or Christ. We don't just
categorize others by their faults and weaknesses; we look deeper. Behind their sometimes unimpressive facade, we see their real
yearnings. In the depths of our hearts all
of us want to be good. We do not deny the
wrong that we see in others, but we do not
condemn them. We try to look beyond the
immediate wrongdoing. We realize that no

one does wrong for pleasure, but rather out of despair, as the psychiatrist Albert Görres once said.

Reverence has to do with respect. We ought not respect people just because of what they achieve but rather because they are human beings. When we feel respected we can take heart. We rediscover our divine dignity. Today I still remember what an Argentinian friend said about my father years ago: "He makes you feel respected." In a strange country, this meant a lot to him, not to be branded an alien but to be respected as a human being. Reverence respects the boundaries the other person wants regarded. It respects another's privacy. We need such Angels of Reverence today at a time when there is a hunger for sensational, intimate details about others' private lives. Reverence creates an atmosphere of delicacy and protectiveness, tenderness and respect, which does us good. With it we really feel like human beings with unassailable dignity.

Reverence has to do with greatness. Today there is an urge to drag what is supposedly great through the dirt. The inferior cannot bear the fact that there is genuine human greatness. They have to spy out its weaknesses, prove to themselves that there cannot be such a thing as human greatness, in order to justify their own mediocrity. When reverent we acknowledge greatness and rejoice in it. And by rejoicing in it, we share in the greatness of what we admire. However, reverence is not only for the great but also for the little, the defenseless, and the injured. Reverence recognizes their divine dignity. This dignity shines from the disfigured face of the tortured. Anyone who exploits another's defenselessness is shameless and humiliates another human being. Reverence does the opposite. It gives people space and freedom to discover their own dignity and take heart.

Today on many occasions, we need Angels of Reverence, to change the climate of cynicism and hunger for sensation into one of respect for human dignity. If an Angel of Reverence ever went to a party, gossip about other people would stop, and an atmosphere of respect would arise, in which all could be themselves, and all would know they were respected. If this Angel turned up at the Town Hall or entered a debate in the City Council, the cruel accusations hurled at members of the opposite party would cease. They would be ruled out of order. If such an Angel of Reverence joined a community, the curiosity that tried to poke its nose into everyone else's secrets would cease. Then we would no longer be constantly trying to change others. We would see each person as their own person and respect them for who they are. Only in an atmosphere of reverence and respect can anyone really change without losing self-respect. When we know our own dignity, we can change and grow to become more like the person inborn in our divine dignity.

My wish for you is that you may live near many Angels of Reverence. Then you will become increasingly aware of the deep mystery within you. You will experience what it means to be human. And you will enjoy your own humanity. I also wish that you may become an Angel of Reverence for others and learn to see your neighbors with the eyes of an Angel of Reverence. Then you will give others space in which they can wholly be themselves.

THE ANGEL
OF UNDERSTANDING

PSYCHOLOGY TRIES TO HEAL us without criticizing, without judging and without condemning us, no matter what we say. When I feel understood I can express everything that is inside of me. I no longer anxiously try to hide things. I feel that with this listener everything is in good hands — this listener understands me and thus enables me to understand myself better. Someone who understands me, without judging or condemning me, has a healing and liberating effect on me. At last I can talk about what has been distressing me for so long, something I have always held back because I was ashamed of it, because it goes against my moral principles. When I speak about it openly to someone else it loses its poisonous effect. I no longer need to use all my energy to hide this unpleasant and unmentionable thing. It comes out of hiding into the light, so it can change.

The word 'understand' comes from 'stand.' The German word for understand is *verstehen*, which also comes from *stehen*, to stand. However, in German the prefix is different. Instead of 'under-', as in English, it is *ver-*, which is related to the Latin *pro* (for), *prae* (before), and *per* (through). Those who 'forestand' (*verstehen*) me stand before me, in front of me, and protect me from the projections others cast upon me. They stand before me, in front of me, so that behind them I can learn to stand myself. They stand by me, so that I can gain a stronger footing in life. They stand by my side through my problems. They do not get weak-kneed when they hear about my weaknesses. By understanding my situation, they also make me able to stand (tolerate and endure) my life. I no longer stumble about, not knowing what is the matter with me. I can stand on my own, because someone else understands me.

In German we say of two friends that they understand each other 'blendend' which means dazzlingly and radiantly. "Getting along like a house on fire" might be an English equivalent of this. I don't just want a friend who understands me, but also someone with whom I understand myself. People who understand each other deeply, who don't have constant misunderstandings, stand on good terms with each other. They stand together. Each allows the other his or her own stand. You can be as you are. You can do as you feel. You do not have to adapt yourself to me. Understanding each other means that neither of us exploits the other for our own ends. However, I can have a good understanding with a friend only if I have gained enough self-knowledge. If I can stand  solid only when the other person is with me, I am dependent. That is against my dignity. In order to understand myself, I need the Angel of Understanding. An Angel who understands me better than I do myself, sees things in me that are still hidden from me or that I do not want to see; sees me clearly without judging me. The Angel of Understanding sees and understands. This enables me to see myself as I am, understand myself, and take responsibility for myself.

Understanding heals. In a pastoral conversation I am always grateful when the other person feels understood. Then there is a feeling of closeness and intensity. Then the other person can take heart. Because when you feel understood, you stand again. You can breathe again. You lose your fear that you are not good enough, that you should not be as you are. You feel firm ground under your feet again. So my wish for you is that you should meet many Angels of Understanding, who give you new standing power. I also wish that you become such an Angel of Understanding for others. You will experience how much good it does you if another person tells you "I feel understood by you. I like being with you. It is good to stand with you. You protect me. Then other people's prejudices don't bother me. I don't have to condemn myself. With you I can stand by myself."

THE ANGEL OF DARKNESS

I F I WISH YOU THE ANGEL OF DARKNESS, I am not wishing that everything around you and in you should become dark. What I am asking is that an Angel visit you and accompany you in your darkness. Sometimes it is dark inside us. Our mood suddenly darkens, and often we do not know where these dark feelings come from. We may think of the future and see only darkness. We are worried how things will go. We may look at a relationship or our marriage, and it is as if we were standing in a dark cloud. Everything feels threatening. We are afraid we will never find our way out of the darkness. If faith has been a light to you on your way, it can happen that suddenly your faith also goes dark, that God hides behind the darkness in your heart.

Many of us today suffer from depressive feelings. In depression everything becomes dark. All that used to give joy slips away. We feel we are sitting in a dark hole and can't get out. In this hole we can't even feel ourselves. Everything becomes numb, meaningless, and dark. The light of human love no longer reaches us. Well-meant words just go over our heads. Loving words sound empty. Words of advice go unheeded and have no effect. We hear the words but don't understand them. They do not reach us. If others try to help us out of a dark hole they may find that they are powerless to do anything. So an Angel must come and climb down into this darkness and reach out a hand to us in our dark nights. Such an Angel must not be afraid of the dark. This angel must be confident not to fall into the black abyss but trust on being well supported. She needs courage to climb down into the dark hole, and sit with us when we are down there.

The Angel of Darkness is also the Angel of Night, the angel who speaks to us in dreams. "At night I'll speak with the angel, if he acknowledges my eyes," writes Rilke in a poem. When we don't know anything anymore, when other people's words no longer reach us, often a dream like this can bring about a turning point. All at once our spirits become lighter. I once accompanied a young woman who had been raped. Nothing I said reached her. All I could do was listen to her pain and distress and dry her tears. Then she dreamed of a playful child who was teasing a giant. Suddenly everything changed. For the first time she felt hope again. She felt alive again and she recovered her will to live. What all my words failed to do, the Angel of Night accomplished through a dream. In the Bible God often sends his Angels to tell people something in a dream, to show them a new way and give them the certainty that God is with them and their life will succeed. Joseph sat in the deep pit with no hope of being saved. But he had been given the certainty in a dream that his life would succeed. The dream brought light into the darkness of the pit. So he did not give up — he hung on to the promise the Angel had given him in his dream. My wish for you is that the Angel of Night will visit you and show you your next step in a dream, to lead you out of darkness and on to the road of freedom and love.

THE ANGEL OF QUIET

ANGELS ARE DELICATE CREATURES. You can't grab hold of them. They come unexpectedly. You must lay yourself open so that you can meet them. Angels come on tiptoes. You need to be very quiet in order to perceive them. There is an Angel who would like to teach you the art of silence, in the healing atmosphere of quiet. In our noisy world we need a lot of quiet, in order to recuperate. Kierkegaard famously said that if he were a doctor he would advise people: "Create silence!" Rabindranath Tagore suggested, "Bathe your soul in silence." Quiet is medicine for the soul, which is often clogged by the noise of the world. The soul can no longer breathe because noisy thoughts and images keep pressing in on it.

Everything great requires quiet in order to be born in us. "Only in silence can genuine knowledge be attained," said Romano Guardini. And Johannes Climacus, a monk in the early Church, said, "Silence is a fruit of wisdom and possesses the knowledge of all things." Silence prepares us to listen well, to hear the nuances in what someone says to us. Silence is necessary in order to hear God's voice in our hearts. Many people today complain that they do not experience God, that God has become a stranger to them. But they are so full of noise they do not hear the still, small impulses through which God speaks in their hearts. We always have something to distract us. As soon as a delicate impulse touches us we shove it aside and turn back to what we can get hold of. So we never hear God's voice.

Stille, the German word meaning quiet, comes from *stillen*, meaning to suckle, quiet, or put to rest. The mother suckles the hungry baby, so that it stops yelling. The Angel of Quiet wants to silence our noisy thoughts, our crying wishes and needs, so that we discover the quiet place inside us. The mystics are convinced that there is a quiet place in each of us, where thoughts and feelings, wishes and needs have no access. It is also the place where people, with their expectations and demands, judgments and condemnations have no access. It is the place in me where I am wholly myself. It is the quiet place, where God himself dwells in me. There, no one can harm me. There, I am safe and sound. Every day I need to sit and meditate. In meditation I imagine how my breath and the word that I connect with my breath lead me into this inner quiet place. To this place people who pass by my office today have no access to that place. There, no one can reach me with their wishes or judgments. There, I can breathe freely. There, I am alone with my God. This gives my life dignity. In this inner quiet place I come into contact with my true self. Quiet changes me. Especially if you have a lot of interaction with other people, if many people want something from you, if you get into intense conversations with them, you need the Angel of Quiet, to silence the countless words in your head that you hear every day. In silence you can draw breath again. You can off-load everything that other people have put onto you. The Angel of Quiet would like to lead you into the inner space, where even the people who you belong to cannot enter. Only when you are in contact with this inner quiet space can you get involved with others without fear. Then you need not be afraid that other people's problems will take you over and demand too much, or that you will be smeared by the dirt you often deal with in conversation.

There is a place where you remain untouched by all the stuff people want to dump on you. In this inner quiet place you remain safe and sound. The Angel of Quiet would like to accompany you and keep reminding you that this place is already exists within you. You do not have to create it. You need only get into touch with the quiet that is in you and can heal you. There, in the space of silence, you can rest. There you are safe and sound. There is something clear and pure in you, which cannot be troubled by the world's noise.

ANSELM GRUEN

is an extremely popular religious writer who has written nearly 300 titles translated into numerous languages, and has sold 14 million copies worldwide.

Fr. Gruen's approach to theology is highly original, yet practical. It combines his profound knowledge of both religion and psychology, with special reference to the psychologist C. G. Jung. He writes books which help others by encouraging them to fully "live their own lives."

Gruen was raised in Munich. At the age of 19 he became a Benedictine monk and later studied Philosophy, Theology and Economics. For many years he was the adminstrator of the abbey of Münsterschwarzach in Southern Germany, where he also directed residential courses in meditation techniques, psychoanalytical interpretation of dreams, fasting, and contemplation, and where he is still a monk.

The abbey was founded in 815 and runs twenty flourishing trades and businesses, including a publishing house, a printshop, a goldsmithy, and a bookshop, all of which make it largely self-supporting, enabling voluntary contributions to be devoted to missionary work.

Anselm Gruen
WISDOM FROM THE DESERT FATHERS
Heaven Begins With You

Masterfully, monk and international best-seller Anselm Gruen reveals the Desert Fathers' surprisingly modern approach to spirituality, relating their passion for God to modern spiritual seeking. The author's profound psychological and theological knowledge offers you deeper insight into your own seach for heaven.

978-0-8245-1818-9, paperback

Abraham Joshua Heschel
I ASKED FOR WONDER
A Spiritual Anthology

One of the most influential Jewish theologians of the 20th century, Heschel captured the sense of mystical wonder in a way few writers can do. This anthology, edited by Rabbi Samuel H. Dresner, presents the finest meditations and insights from Heschel's bountiful writing

978-0-8245-0542-4, paperback

Luellen Hoffman
SPECIAL DREAM
Personal Accounts After the Death of a Loved One

Ask anyone who has experienced a special dream—a vivid encounter with a loved one who has died—and you'll hear the same words: "It was unlike any other dream." Hoffman lifts the veil of mystery by sharing the healing they offer.

978-0-8245-2541-5, paperback